BEGINNER'S GUIDE TO STARTING AN ETSY PRINT ON DEMAND SHOP

How To Start Your Own POD Business Selling Clothing, Home Décor & More

BY ANN ECKHART

TABLE OF CONTENTS

INTRODUCTION

Etsy is known as a handmade marketplace, an online space for artists and crafters to sell their wares. Etsy also features shops filled with antiques and vintage collectibles. But did you know that there is a completely different category of product on Etsy, one that is earning sellers over six figures a year?

It's called print-on-demand, or POD for short. In this business model, products are not produced (printed) until an order is placed (demand). While some refer to this process as "drop shipping," it is a different business structure.

In a drop shipping business model, an online store doesn't keep the inventory they sell in stock. Rather, when a product sells, they purchase the item from a third party and have it shipped directly to the customer. The customer is unaware that the product didn't come from the store they ordered it from. Electronics are one of the biggest categories in drop shipping. For example, that cheap toaster you ordered through an eBay store that lists hundreds of the same version for sale is likely a drop shipping business.

In a print-on-demand business model, however, an online store creates graphics for its products. Things such as graphic tee shirts, coffee mugs, and even books. They then place these graphics on products through a print-on-demand printer and list the products for sale online. If you have ever browsed Amazon and seen graphic tee shirts for sale, they are almost always part of the Merch by Amazon program where sellers load graphics onto tee shirts that Amazon supplies. When an order is placed, Amazon prints the shirt and ships it to the customer. Amazon products are all print-on-demand.

Drop shipping products are sold as-is. Print-on-demand products require the seller to create graphics and files to be printed onto products. They list these products online, and when a customer places an order, the manufacturer of the product prints it and ships it. Unlike drop shipping where products are all ready to go, print-on-demand products required extra steps.

The book you are reading right now is a print-on-demand book. I authored this book, uploaded the file to Amazon, and when you ordered it, Amazon printed and shipped it to you. Or if you are reading the eBook version, they send the file to your reading device. I didn't ship you a copy of this book; Amazon did. But it is my work, my writing, my copyrighted material. Amazon is simply the print-on-demand provider I used to print and ship it to you. Amazon takes a cut of the profits, and they distribute the rest to me.

While Amazon is the place to self-publish print-on-demand books (check out my book *Beginner's Guide To Amazon KDP* if you are interested in that topic) and for graphic tee shirts via Merch by Amazon, Etsy has become the top website for selling other print-on-demand products including not only tee shirts and other tops that Amazon sells but also coffee mugs, leggings, pet products, stationery, home décor, and more.

Why would you choose Etsy over Amazon for this business model? The truth is many print-on-demand sellers sell on both sites. After all, you can't deny Amazon's reach as the number one shopping website. But with a print-on-demand Etsy shop, you can offer not only shirts but many other products. And an Etsy shop allows you to build your brand. Unlike Amazon, where most customers never look at a seller's store, on Etsy, customers typically check out a seller's shop, meaning you have more opportunities to sell other products.

However, there is one major difference between Merch by Amazon and an Etsy print-on-demand shop: While Amazon prints and ships orders, Etsy does not. Rather Etsy sellers must connect to a third-part company to produce their products. Here's how it works:

- Sellers create an account with a third-party print provider.
- Sellers then link that account to their Etsy shop.
- Sellers create designs and upload them to the third-party print provider and choose which products they want the designs to appear on.
- The products then integrate into the seller's Etsy shop.
- When an item sells, the print-on-demand provider prints and ships the product to the customer.

Sounds easy, doesn't it? While the process sounds simple, building a successful Etsy print-on-demand shop, which is what we will cover in this book, takes more time and effort than most realize. But the work you need to put into starting and growing a POD brand on Etsy has several advantages over the other POD websites, including Amazon. In fact, Etsy has become the most popular platform for this business model. Some reasons for this include:

1. **Targeted audience:** Etsy has a unique and dedicated audience of shoppers who are interested in items they can't find anywhere else and that are very niche, making it a good fit for sellers of personalized and custom products as well as items targeted at specific shoppers.
2. **Lower fees:** Etsy charges lower fees than Amazon, which can be beneficial for small businesses and startups. In fact, a print-on-demand Etsy shop offers one of the lowest start-up costs of any online business today. For under $50 a month, you can build up an Etsy POD business that may bring in a full-time level income.
3. **Strong brand identity:** With over 60 million active buyers worldwide, Etsy has a strong brand identity and a well-established reputation as a safe marketplace. This gives sellers a built-in advantage when it comes to launching their businesses as they aren't going to have to bring customers to Etsy. The customer base is already there.

4. **More control over the customer experience:** On Etsy, sellers can create their shops using color schemes and designs that fit their brand and help attract customers who are drawn to their unique aesthetic. With careful planning, you can build your Etsy shop to target a specific customer base who loves your design and product selection.
5. **Features:** Etsy offers sellers numerous built-in features to customize their shops and create unique listings. From the ability to add videos and customization options to handling payment and remitting sales tax to the US states that require it, Etsy allows its sellers to focus on running their businesses while they take care of the back-end technicalities.

This book will walk you step-by-step through the entire process of starting and growing an Etsy print-on-demand shop. Note that I will usually reference print-on-demand as POD. We'll cover everything you need to know including:

- Equipment needed to run a print-on-demand business.
- The different print-on-demand providers and how to choose the ones that best fit your business.
- How to research the various niches.
- Deciding which print-on-demand products you want to sell.
- How to create print-on-demand images for your products.
- How to open your Etsy shop.
- How to integrate your POD provider into your Etsy shop.
- How to create your POD Etsy listings.
- How to process orders.
- Marketing and advertising strategies to bring customers to your shop.
- How to handle customer service issues.
- How to manage your Etsy shop's bookkeeping.
- How to grow your POD business beyond Etsy.

With just a computer and internet connection, anyone can start an Etsy print-on-demand shop. So. if you are ready to learn everything there is to know about this exciting home-based business, let's get started!

CHAPTER ONE: ESSENTIAL EQUIPMENT FOR AN ETSY POD SHOP

We covered the basics of print-on-demand in the Introduction to this book. But to actually start a POD business, you need some essential equipment. Well, you only need ONE piece of equipment: a computer!

However, not just any computer will do. You will need a rather powerful computer if you want to grow a POD shop. Between creating graphics, downloading files, and having multiple websites open at once on your screen, a quality computer is necessary to work quickly and efficiently. Because a computer is the main component of running a POD business, it will be getting a lot of wear and tear.

You can certainly start with the computer you already have, but don't be surprised if you need to eventually upgrade. If you find you need a more powerful computer to run your business, here are some specifications you want to look for:

Operating System: The operating system is the software that manages the hardware and software resources of a computer. For an Etsy print-on-demand shop, either Windows 10 or MacOS (the latest version) can be used as the operating system.

To simplify this, note that PCs (non-Apple brands) run on Windows, while Apple brands run on Mac. Artists who design their own images for print-on-demand typically use Apple products, including iPads and Apple Pencils. However, I have always run all my online businesses, including print-on-demand, on a PC. It is a matter of personal preference.

Processor: The processor, also known as the central processing unit (CPU), is the primary component that performs calculations and executes instructions on a computer. For an Etsy print-on-demand shop, a powerful processor with the following specifications is recommended:

- **Intel Core i5 or equivalent:** An Intel Core i5 processor provides a good balance of processing power and energy efficiency. It is suitable for most tasks involved in running a print-on-demand shop, including when you use design software and web browsing.
- **Clock speed:** A clock speed of 2.0 GHz or higher is recommended for an Intel Core i5 processor.
- **Multiple cores:**Multi-core processors can handle multiple tasks simultaneously, improving performance and efficiency. Since a POD business means you will often have multiple programs running at once, a dual-core or quad-core processor is recommended.

RAM: RAM (Random Access Memory) is a type of computer memory that temporarily stores data and is used to improve a computer's performance. For an Etsy print-on-demand shop, the following RAM specifications are recommended:

- **8 GB or higher:** 8 GB of RAM provides enough memory for most tasks involved in running a print-on-demand shop, such as web browsing and using design software. I always recommend getting the most RAM you can afford.
- **DDR4 or DDR5:** DDR4 or DDR5 RAM is the latest generation of memory and provides improved performance and energy efficiency compared to older generations.

In the context of an Etsy print-on-demand shop, RAM is important because it allows the computer to handle multiple tasks and applications simultaneously. This is essential for managing orders, uploading product images, communicating with customers, and running design and image editing software.

If a computer has insufficient RAM, it can slow down or freeze when running multiple applications or tasks, making it difficult to manage your business efficiently. A larger amount of RAM provides more space for the processor to store data and information, which can improve overall performance and speed.

Storage: Storage refers to the permanent or semi-permanent memory on a computer where data is saved. For an Etsy print-on-demand shop, the following storage specifications are recommended:

- **256 GB SSD or higher:** A solid-state drive (SSD) is a type of storage that provides fast read and write speeds, improving the overall performance of the computer. 256 GB SSD provides enough space to store the shop's operating system, applications, and a moderate amount of data.
- **Large files:** Design files and product images can be large, so it's recommended to have additional storage in the form of an external hard drive or cloud storage.

When it comes to computer storage for an Etsy print-on-demand shop, it is important to have as much possible to accommodate the images and designs for the products you are selling, as well as any additional files or information you need to store on your system. As your business grows, you will need more storage space to handle the increasing number of graphic files.

Graphics: A graphics card (also known as a GPU) is a component in a computer that is responsible for rendering images and video. For an Etsy print-on-demand shop, a dedicated graphics card is not typically required. However, a good integrated graphics card can improve the performance of a computer, especially if the shop owner uses design software that requires a lot of graphical processing. Good options for graphics cards include:

- **Intel UHD Graphics or NVIDIA GeForce:** Integrated graphics cards, such as Intel UHD Graphics or NVIDIA GeForce, can provide reliable performance for most tasks involved in running a print-on-demand shop.
- **Dedicated graphics card:** If a POD shop owner uses resource-intensive design software or plans to use their system to also play high-end games, a dedicated graphics card may be required. In such cases, a NVIDIA GeForce or AMD Radeon graphics card is recommended.

Display: Etsy POD shop owners spend most of their time in front of their computer screens. I use a laptop computer, and I always look for the largest screen I can find as it makes designing graphics much easier. The following display specifications are recommended for an Etsy POD shop:

- **Screen size:** A screen size of at least 15 inches is recommended for a desktop computer. A laptop computer with a screen size of 13-14 inches is suitable for most tasks involved in running a print-on-demand shop.
- **Resolution:** A resolution of 1920x1080 or higher provides clear and sharp images and text and graphics. Higher resolutions may be required if the shop owner uses design software that requires a lot of screen real estate.
- **Display type:** A display with an IPS panel provides good viewing angles and accurate colors, which is important for design work. Note that the specific display requirements will depend on the other components of the computer and the specific software used.

Internet Connection: An internet connection is essential for running an Etsy print-on-demand shop. You will need fast, safe, and reliable internet service to connect to graphics websites, access online design services, and integrate your print provider into your Etsy shop. The following internet connection specifications are recommended for an Etsy POD business:

- **Broadband:** A broadband connection, such as cable, fiber, or DSL, provides fast and reliable internet speeds.
- **Speed:** A minimum download speed of 25 Mbps is recommended for running an Etsy print-on-demand shop. This speed provides enough bandwidth to handle the shop's daily tasks, such as uploading product images, processing orders, and communicating with customers.
- **Reliability:** A reliable internet connection ensures that you can access the internet and your Etsy shop's resources without interruption. The faster the internet connection, the faster you will be able to design new products and process orders. You also want to have a backup internet connection, such as a mobile hotspot, in case of outages or failures. I use the hotspot on my iPhone for times when my internet goes out.

A print-on-demand business means you will be constantly online dealing with multiple programs. A powerful computer will help you save time when performing the following tasks:

Design software: Whether you are drawing your own graphics or downloading them from a site like Creative Fabrica, a powerful computer is necessary to handle graphics-intensive software like Adobe Illustrator or Photoshop.

Multitasking: Running multiple applications and web browsers at the same time can be demanding on the computer's resources. A powerful computer can handle multitasking more effectively, reducing lag and increasing efficiency. When I am working on my Etsy POD shop, I often have Printify, Etsy, Canva, Creative Fabrica, and Keyword Trend all open at the same time. I need a powerful computer to run many programs at once without crashing.

Large files: Design files and product images are large and will slow down a computer if it doesn't have enough processing power and storage. A powerful computer can handle large files with ease.

That being said, a less powerful computer can still be used to start a print-on-demand Etsy shop, but you may experience slower performance or longer wait times when using design software or handling large files. However, to grow, you will want the fastest computer you can afford.

If you want to keep your existing computer running smoothly for your Etsy print-on-demand shop, there are several things you can do:

1. **Keep your operating system and software up to date: Regularly** updating your operating system and software can help improve performance and security.
2. **Uninstall unused software:** Uninstalling software that is not needed can help free up resources and improve performance.
3. **Clean up your hard drive:** Regularly cleaning up your hard drive can help improve performance by freeing up space and reducing fragmentation.
4. **Run virus scans:** Running virus scans regularly can help protect your computer from malware and other security threats.
5. **Add more RAM:** Adding more RAM can help improve performance, especially if your computer has limited memory.
6. **Upgrade your graphics card:** Upgrading your graphics card can help improve performance, especially if you use resource-intensive design software. It's important to note that these tips may not be applicable or may only provide limited improvement for all computers, depending on the specific model and configuration. If your computer continues to experience performance issues, it may be necessary to invest in a new model.

So far, we have discussed the important specifications for the computer that is needed for running an Etsy print-on-demand shop. However, there are a few more things that you will need to set up your POD business. The good news is that everything you need can be found online. You do not have to worry about investing in physical inventory or shipping supplies, as all your work will be done through the internet. This means that you have the flexibility to work from anywhere as long as you have a laptop and a reliable internet connection. Whether you prefer to work from a local coffee shop or a beach on the other side of the world, you can manage and grow your business with ease, making an Etsy print-on-demand shop a perfect opportunity for digital nomads.

So, you have your computer and internet connection. Now it's on to the next step, which is choosing your POD print provider or providers.

CHAPTER TWO: CHOOSING PRINT-ON-DEMAND PROVIDERS

While a computer is the one piece of physical equipment you will need to run an Etsy print-on-demand shop, there are other online-only websites you will need to utilize for your business. The biggest of which is the print-on-demand provider or providers you want to use.

Remember that with print-on-demand, you will be applying graphics to products and linking those products to your Etsy shop. The products will be printed and shipped by your third-party print-on-demand provider. So, you will need an account with a print provider along with your Etsy shop account.

We will cover setting up your Etsy account and shop later on in this book. But first, we need to go over choosing a print provider or providers. I say "providers" in plural because some shops use two or more.

There are several print-on-demand companies that are popular among Etsy sellers for running their POD shops, including:

Printify: Printify is the most popular POD platform for Etsy shop owners. It offers the widest range of products, including clothing, home decor, and accessories. It is the company I personally use for my POD shop as it offers the best products, prices, and service, including the fastest shipping.

One of the key features of Printify is its integration with some of the most popular e-commerce platforms, including Etsy but also eBay, Shopify, WooCommerce, and recently Walmart, making it easy for businesses to not only set up and run their POD Etsy shop but also expand as they grow.

With Printify, you can manage your product designs and orders from a single platform, and have your products printed and shipped directly to your customers. Printify offers a wide range of products to choose from, including:

- **Apparel:** T-shirts, tank tops, hoodies, sweatshirts, and dresses
- **Home Decor:** Posters, canvas prints, throw pillows, and Christmas ornaments
- **Accessories:** Phone cases, tote bags, hats, and socks
- **Stationery:** Notebooks, journals, stickers, and magnets
- **Drinkware:** Mugs, water bottles, and tumblers
- **Bags:** Backpacks, duffel bags, weekender bags, and purses
- **Pet Products:** Pet beds, bandanas, pet feeding mats, collars, and leashes

Printify offers a variety of printing methods, including screen printing, digital printing, and sublimation, to ensure that you can find the best option for your designs. It also provides a live preview of your designs on different products, so you can see how your designs will look before you decide to create a listing.

Another benefit of using Printify is its network of print providers, which allows you to choose from a variety of various products from suppliers across the globe, narrowing down your selections based on each printer's ranking, product cost, and shipping charge. This is really what sets Printify apart because they aren't the printer but rather connect you with printers across the globe.

For me, I prefer to use print providers based in the United States. Since I am based in the U.S. and only ship within the U.S. this means my customers will get their orders much faster than if I used overseas providers. I recommend that you look for print providers within the country of your business, or as close to it as possible. Because POD products aren't printed until an order is placed, it takes longer to not only produce these items but also for them to ship to the customer. Choosing providers within your country will help reduce the shipping time.

I also search for providers based on their feedback. Sellers can rank the various providers and their products on a scale of one to ten. I look for U.S.-based printers with a score of no lower than eight to ensure that the products, quality, and shipping are the best possible.

PRO TIP: Note that during the busy holiday season, the ratings on Printify's providers tend to dip due to orders taking longer to fulfill and ship. This is due to the huge increase in production and isn't always a reflection of the quality of the products. I try to give providers the benefit of the doubt during the Christmas shopping season, especially if they usually have a much higher rating but are slipping a bit. Ratings always get back to normal in January.

Printify offers both a free and a paid subscription. The free subscription provides access to all product options; however, there is a markup on the wholesale price. The paid subscription offers discounted pricing, with a monthly fee for access to lower costs. If you want to grow a POD business, you will want to upload to their Premium option as the 20% discount will more than make up for the cost.

Printful: Like Printify, Printful is a comprehensive print-on-demand company that provides a range of products and printing services for businesses, including t-shirts, hoodies, mugs, phone cases, and more. It runs neck-and-neck with Printify as the most popular of the POD companies in the market and is popular with Etsy sellers looking to start a POD business.

In addition to integrating with Etsy and Shopify, Printful also integrates with Amazon. This is a huge plus for those looking to expand their POD business beyond Etsy as Amazon is the biggest e-commerce website in most countries, specifically America.

Printful offers high-quality printing services and a wide range of products to choose from, including:

- **Apparel:** T-shirts, hoodies, sweatshirts, and leggings
- **Home Decor:** Posters, canvas prints, and throw pillows
- **Accessories:** Phone cases, tote bags, and hats
- **Stationery:** Notebooks, journals, stickers, and calendars
- **Drinkware:** Mugs, water bottles, and tumblers
- **Bags:** Backpacks, duffel bags, and tote bags
- **Pet Products:** Pet beds, bandanas, and feeding mats
- **Outdoor:** Beach towels, picnic blankets, and flags

As with Printify, Printful offers a variety of printing methods, including direct-to-garment printing, sublimation, and embroidery, to ensure that you can find the best option for your designs. It also provides a mockup generator, which allows you to see how your designs will look on various products before you create a listing.

Additionally, both Printify and Printful provide customization options for product designs, including the ability to add text, images, and custom graphics to your products. Printful also offers fast and reliable shipping, with products shipped directly to customers from its fulfillment centers in the United States, Europe, and Mexico. It provides various shipping options, including standard and express shipping, so you can choose the best options for your business.

Just as with Printify, Printful offers a free version as well as paid monthly subscription plans. While there is no discount with the paid version, you do get access to added features, including:

- **Priority Support:** Faster response times from the Printful support team.
- **Customized Fulfillment:** Custom branding options, including custom packing slips, packaging, and more.
- **Product Insights:** Advanced analytics and reporting tools to help you track your business's performance and make informed decisions.

- **Product Sampling:** Access to Printful's product sampling program allows you to request samples of products before making a bulk order.
- **Access to Private Products:** A wider range of products that are not available to the public, including some premium products.

Unlike Printify, which gives you 20% off when you upgrade to a paid subscription, there is no reason to pay for Printful until you have grown your POD business to a level where you feel you need the extra features.

Printify vs. Printful: Most Etsy POD shops use Printify, Printful, or a combination of both. This is the beauty of a POD business in that you can use multiple suppliers to access the products you want. For example, Printify offers more sticker options than Printful; but Printful offers more clothing options. And there are numerous products that both sites offer, but sometimes an item is cheaper on one or ranked higher on the other.

When you have a POD shop, you will want to research the best products for value, quality, and shipping. Fortunately, both Printify and Printful offer a rating system, which can help you decide which site to use for each product you sell.

Both Printify and Printful operate on a cost-plus pricing model, which means that they add a markup to the cost of production and shipping. The cost of selling products from these sties includes several different fees:

1. **Base product price:** This is the cost of producing each item, which includes the cost of materials and manufacturing. This price varies depending on the product and the printing method.
2. **Printing fee:** This fee is charged for each product printed and varies depending on the printing method, product type, and quantity.
3. **Shipping fee:** This fee covers the cost of shipping the product to the customer. The cost of shipping varies depending on the product's weight, size, and shipping destination.

4. **Platform fee:** Printify charges a platform fee, which is a percentage of the total sale price, for using their service. This fee ranges from 10% to 20% depending on the plan you choose.

It is important to note that these fees are subject to change and may vary depending on factors such as product type, shipping destination, and volume. Additionally, the cost of products is not fixed, as the cost of production and shipping can fluctuate over time. It is important to regularly review and compare costs to ensure that you are staying competitive in the market.

The payment of fees for Printify and Printful typically works as follows: When you make a sale through your Etsy POD shop that is fulfilled by Printify, Printful, or another provider, the cost of the product and the cost for the provider to ship the product to your customer is added to your account balance. All POD printers require sellers to place a credit card on file; these costs are then added to your card every time a new order is placed.

When you make a POD sale on Etsy, Etsy will deposit the profit (after their fees and shipping costs) into your Etsy account. You then use that money to pay for the fees and costs associated with using Printify or Printful to fulfill the order, including the product cost and shipping. What is left after these expenses are paid is your final net profit.

Let's say you sell a sweatshirt on Etsy through Printify. The sweatshirt cost $20 to produce and $5 to ship. Printify will charge your credit card $25. You had the sweatshirt listed on Etsy for $40 with the buyer paying the $5 shipping cost for a total of $45. After Etsy takes out its fees, you would have $40.27 left in your Etsy account balance. You would then withdraw that money to your checking account and pay the $25 Printify charged to your credit card. You would then be left with $15.27 in profit from the sale.

PRO TIP: I use an Etsy Fee Calculator to make sure I understand all the fees associated with each POD product I list. There are many free calculators available online; my favorite is https://omniprofitcalculator.com/etsy-fee-calculator/.

While Printify and Printful are the most popular POD print providers, there are a few others you may want to consider:

Teelaunch: Teelaunch is another print-on-demand platform that allows you to create and sell custom products online through their Etsy integration. It is similar to Printify and Printful in that it handles production, shipping, and customer service. But Teelaunch differs from Printify and Printful in terms of one main product and that is jewelry, including necklaces, bracelets, and earrings, that can be customized with your designs. Other unique products include yard flags, sports balls, wood-cutting boards, and plates.

Gooten: Gooten offers a range of products similar to Printful and Printify, including clothing, home decor, accessories, and personalized gifts. Gooten has a wider range of product categories compared to Printful and Printify, including more items for the home and kitchen. Additionally, Gooten offers different customization options, such as 3D printing, laser engraving, and sublimation printing.

Gearbubble: Gearbubble is a print-on-demand company that specializes in unique and customizable products, such as phone cases, jewelry, home decor, and accessories. Gearbubble's focus on specialty items and the ability to add personal touches, like custom text and designs, make them a popular choice for sellers looking to offer unique products. Additionally, Gearbubble has a user-friendly interface for creating and uploading designs, making it easy for even those with little design experience to get started.

Ordering Samples: Almost all POD providers, including Printify and Printful, allow you to order samples of your products or purchase them in large quantities to use as giveaways or to sell yourself. While the beauty of POD is that you don't have to carry inventory or ship orders yourself, having some of your physical products on hand to showcase in videos, to use in exchange for reviews, or even to sell locally if your business grows is something to think about. Ordering samples is also a nice way to see your products in person and evaluate the quality yourself.

CHAPTER THREE: SELECTING YOUR NICHE & PRODUCTS

You now know that you need a powerful computer and a high-speed internet connection to start an Etsy print-on-demand shop. And we've covered some of the different print providers available. Now comes the fun part: Deciding on your niche and what products you want to sell!

Niche refers to a specific and well-defined market segment or a particular area of interest that has a specific target audience. Niches are important for Etsy POD shops because they help the shop to focus its product offerings and marketing efforts that target a select group of customers.

An Etsy POD business isn't like Walmart or Amazon where you are offering products for all ages, genders, and interests. Instead, you want to focus on targeting specific niches of customers who are looking for specific products.

The best-selling niches for print-on-demand on Etsy or any e-commerce platform can vary depending on many factors such as current trends, market demand, and competition. However, some of the most popular niches include:

- Pop culture references
- Pets, especially cat and dog-related products
- Humor, including witty slogans and memes
- Fitness, wellness, and yoga
- Personalized products, such as monograms and custom names
- Nature and outdoor-related products
- Home decor, including throw pillows and wall art
- Travel and adventure-themed products
- Quotes and motivational sayings

It's worth noting that these niches can be further sub-divided into smaller, more specific niches to target specific customer groups. For instance, you could narrow down the travel niche to offer customized cruise ship door magnets or create duffle bags for lesser knows sports.

So, which niche should you target? Can you only target one niche or target multiple niches in the same Etsy shop?

Most successful Etsy shops focus on one niche per store. And that right there is a key: I said store, as in singular. You can target different niches, but it is best to focus on one niche per store. Yes, you can have multiple Etsy shops. Many successful POD Etsy businesses eventually expand to have multiple stores for different niches. Perhaps they started with a store targeting bridal shoppers but then opened a new shop targeting pet owners.

But starting your POD journey, you will want to focus on one store with one niche. Here are some examples of niche-specific Etsy shops:

- A shop focused on pet-related products such as custom dog shirts and cat beds.
- A shop focused on custom jewelry for bridal parties
- A shop focused on eco-friendly reusable canvas grocery bags
- A shop focused on kitchen accessories such as potholders and aprons
- A shop that only sells Halloween-themed tee shirts
- A shop that only sells personalized Christmas ornaments

As you look over these niche examples, what ideas are coming to your mind? Do you love dogs and would like to focus on pet collars and leashes? Are you a fitness buff who would love to develop your own line of workout tees and leggings? Perhaps you are a home cook who would like to create designs for cutting boards and oven mitts.

The potential for creating products for different niches is only limited by your imagination. However, before you commit to a niche, there's one thing you need to understand, and that is trademark infringement.

Trademark Infringement: Trademark infringement is a serious issue for all print-on-demand businesses, as it involves using someone else's registered trademark or intellectual property in your designs or products without their permission. This can, at worst, lead to legal consequences, but more often than not, will result in you losing your selling account on whatever platform you are selling on.

How do you check to see if a design or phrase is trademarked?

The US Patent and Trademark Office (USPTO) is a government agency responsible for granting patents for new inventions and registering trademarks for product and service names and logos. The website https://www.uspto.gov/trademarks is the USPTO's official website for trademark information, including searching for existing trademarks, filing a trademark application, and managing a trademark after it is registered.

As a POD shop owner, you will want to check every design on the USPTO website before you list it on Etsy. Listing an item that violates someone else's trademark can result in cease-and-desist orders, fines, or even legal action. At the very least, Etsy will remove your listings. At worst, they will permanently terminate your account.

Some common examples of trademark infringement you will see on Etsy include:

- Producing and selling products with Disney characters like Mickey Mouse, Frozen, and Cinderella

- Making and selling products with Marvel characters like Spider-Man, Iron Man, and Captain America
- Selling products with Star Wars logos, images, and characters like Darth Vader and the Galactic Empire symbol
- Creating and selling products with NFL team logos, such as the New England Patriots, Green Bay Packers, and Dallas Cowboys
- Producing and selling products with the logos and branding of popular movies and TV shows, like Harry Potter, Game of Thrones, and The Simpsons.
- Using music song quotes
- Using the likenesses of celebrities

It is shocking to me how many people do not know about trademark infringement. Yet every day, Etsy Facebook groups and other online Etsy forums are filled with posts from sellers who have had their listings pulled, or worse, their accounts terminated because they violated a trademark.

While searching the website https://www.uspto.gov/trademarks will give you the definite answer to whether a phrase is trademarked, note that you need to be aware of images, too. The Nike swish, the McDonald's arches, and even smiley faces are all licensed and cannot be used in POD products, even if you aren't using the brand names.

The first step to identifying trademarks is to ask yourself if someone else created the design. Movies, music, books, actors, singers, writers, television shows, song lyrics, and quotes are almost all trademarked. If someone else wrote it, sang it, or made it, it is likely trademarked. And if something is trademarked, you cannot use it.

One of the biggest themes you will see on Etsy is handmade Disney products. From clothing and décor to stickers and stationery, there are thousands of Disney-themed products for sale on Etsy. However, these are all in violation of the trademark as only Disney is authorized to create and sell Disney products. Unless a seller has gotten express written permission from Disney to sell designs based on the Mouse, they are violating Disney's trademark.

But wait, I know what you are about to say: If these Disney products violate the trademark, how are sellers getting away with selling them?

The fact is that Etsy will rarely pull an item due to trademark infringement on its own. Instead, they wait until the trademark owner alerts them to listings. Disney periodically will go through the site and tell Etsy to take down listings. So, some sellers will go for quite a while selling Disney-looking items. Eventually, however, those listings will be pulled. And worse, you may find yourself in legal hot water with Disney directly.

Etsy generally has a "three strikes and you're out" policy. If you rack up three trademark violations, Etsy will usually terminate your account. And once your account is terminated, it is gone forever. You cannot create a new selling account as you must register using your identity and whatever government issue ID you have in your country (in America, this will be your social security number). And since you only have one ID, you cannot create a second account. Some websites even prohibit a user with the same address, meaning you can't have your spouse create an account to replace the one you lost.

You may be thinking that you can simply create designs that are similar but not exactly like trademarked brands. But a company such as Disney has thousands of trademarks that cover everything from the shape of Mickey Mouse's ears to random messages that play in the theme parks. Many Disney-themed shops will say their products are Disney-inspired. But it doesn't matter; they are still violating Disney's trademark.

Violating another company's trademark is the fastest way to lose your Etsy business before you even sell one item. Ignore the fact that other sellers are violating the rules and instead make sure you aren't!

So, if you can't sell Disney-themed or other pop culture-inspired products, what kinds of designs can you sell? After all, aren't most things trademarked?

The answer is no, most designs aren't trademarked. You just need to be creative in the types of themes you offer. You can't use Disney designs, but you can create travel and vacation-themed designs. You can't use quotes from songs, but you can come up with your own unique sayings. You can't use a celebrity's image, but you can create your own characters.

Research: If you are an artist who wants to turn your designs into images for shirts, mugs, and other products, it is still important to research the market and get a sense of what is trending to ensure that your products will be appealing to shoppers. You may love designing flowers, for example; but knowing which flowers are the most sought after – say, sunflowers versus roses - will give you a leg up on the competition.

On the other hand, if you are someone who has no idea about what designs to create but wants to start a POD business, you may need to purchase graphics from other designers. This is quite common when it comes to POD. Most Etsy POD shops purchase their images outright while others do some editing to images.

But before you can even think about designing or purchasing graphics, you need to figure out the niche you want to target. And to do that, you will need to do some research.

Etsy: The first place you want to start when it comes to researching POD niches is Etsy itself. After all, it is the top platform for POD products. Browse through the various categories and see what types of products are popular. Pay attention to the number of sales, the number of items in the category, and the overall engagement of the category.

Use the Etsy search bar to look for keywords related to your niche. You can add filters such as "most recent" or "most relevant" to narrow down your results. Analyze the top results for each keyword you search. Take note of the products that are consistently appearing on the first page of search results. This could indicate that these products are in high demand.

Look at the sales and reviews of the top products. See what people are saying about the products and the seller. Check the seller's shop policies, shipping times, and return policies. Take note of the price range of the products in the niche. Consider if there is room for profit in the niche and if you can offer comparable products at a competitive price.

Finally, consider your own skills and interests when choosing a niche. Do you have the resources and knowledge to create and sell products in this niche? Do you have a passion for the niche?

For a more detailed example, let's say you want to research the bridal niche:

1. Visit Etsy and search for "bridal shower gifts" or "bridal gifts".
2. Take note of the top results, including product titles, tags, and product descriptions.
3. Check out the most popular items and their sellers.
4. Analyze the product descriptions, the photos, the prices, and the shop's shipping policies.
5. Check out the product reviews and ratings. See what customers like and dislike about the products.
6. Repeat the process for different keywords related to the bridal niche, such as "wedding favors", "wedding accessories", etc.
7. Analyze the data collected to determine the most profitable and in-demand products in the bridal niche and then see where you can fill a void in the market that isn't being met.

Visiting local stores to research POD niches can be a clever idea as it allows you to see what products are popular and in demand in your local market. Additionally, you can also gather information about the types of materials, colors, and patterns that are currently popular.

Also, visit the websites of the stores and read reviews of the products. Observe what customers like and dislike about the items they bought. Take note of their suggestions for improvements and apply the insights to your products. Reviews can provide valuable information on what works and what doesn't.

Be sure to look at the clearance sections of both brick-and-mortar stores and websites. After all, if the item is on clearance, it means most people didn't want it at full price. Take note of the colors and designs that fill the clearance racks and cross those niches off your list.

By narrowing down your POD offerings and targeting a specific niche, you will be more likely to identify and fill a void in the market, as well as command higher prices for your products. While basic tee shirts and water bottles are readily available, offering specialized designs for a particular group of people can give you an edge in the market. After all, you can buy a white tee shirt anywhere. But a tee shirt for nursing students who love coffee and cats isn't something you see in Target.

Think of all of the separate ways people characterize themselves, including:

- Gender
- Age
- Sexuality
- Relationship status
- Hometown
- Current location
- Pets
- Family
- Religion
- Politics
- Education
- Career
- Hobbies
- Interests
- Personality traits

How can you create products that target these different niches? A new mom who lives in the Midwest and loves to bake is quite different from a retiree in Florida who loves to take cruise vacations. The types of products these two people buy are vastly different.

Consider your passions and interests, as well as your daily life, to identify opportunities for creating unique and specialized designs. For instance, if you're a gardener, consider focusing on botanical-themed shirts or bags. If you work in the medical field, think about creating designs featuring humorous phrases used by healthcare professionals for water bottles and tote bags they use on the job. If you are a teacher, think about all of the products you and your fellow educators use and see if you can fill a void.

Pinterest: Pinterest is a social media platform that allows users to create and share collections of images and ideas. You can use Pinterest to search for specific types of products or themes and see what other users are pinning and sharing. This can give you a sense of what types of products are popular and inspire your product development.

To use Pinterest to research current POD trends:

1. Go to the Pinterest website (https://www.pinterest.com/) and create an account if you don't already have one. I will discuss using Pinterest to promote your Etsy shop later in this book, so go ahead and create an account now as you will want to use the site to attract customers. It's free and easy to do.
2. In the search bar at the top of the page, enter a relevant search term, such as "bridesmaid gifts" or "teacher gifts."
3. Click the "Search" button.
4. Scroll through the search results to see the most popular pins related to your search term.
5. As you see pins you like, remember to save them to your board, which you can make private. This will allow you to save your research results without anyone else seeing them.
6. Click on individual pins to see more details and to view the source of the pin. If it is an online shop, click through to the store and look at the products they offer.

You can also use Pinterest's "Explore" feature to discover new trends and ideas:

1. Click on the "Explore" icon (a compass) at the top of the Pinterest homepage.
2. Scroll through the "Explore" feed to see popular pins and boards related to your search terms.
3. Click on individual pins or boards to see more details and to view the source of the pin or board, saving them to review.

You can use the search and explore features to find inspiration and ideas for your products and to see what is currently popular on the platform. Keep in mind that the popularity of certain trends may vary based on the location and audience of the users who are using Pinterest.

Paid Tools: Etsy, Pinterest, and retail stores are free and easy ways to research trends. However, there are several third-party tools available that can be useful for researching and analyzing products and trends on Etsy, especially POD products. These tools can provide insights into things like sales history, search ranking, and competition within specific niches.

Using a paid tool isn't a requirement for building a successful Etsy POD shop, but it can come in handy, especially if you have no idea of the types of products you want to sell. Most of these sites offer free trials and then month-to-month subscriptions so that you can test them out before deciding if you want to commit to a paid plan.

Some examples of paid third-party tools for Etsy research include:

eRank.com: eRank is a tool that allows you to see the search rankings of specific keywords and products on Etsy. It can help you understand how your products and keywords are performing on the platform and how they compare to other sellers.

I use eRank for researching trends on Etsy. I have a Pro subscription that I pay for on a month-to-month basis, and I have my own Etsy shop synced so that I can get customized data. By typing keywords into eRank's search bar, the site shows me what customers are shopping for and what the competition for that keyword is. I can then decide whether that is a niche I wish to target. If there is too much competition, I will try to further narrow down that niche or skip it altogether in favor of one that is less competitive.

For example, a search for "bridesmaid shirts" will yield dozens of results with stiff competition. However, I see that there isn't nearly as much competition for "funny bridesmaid shirts." I would head over to Etsy and search for "funny bridesmaid shirts" to see what the listings look like and to see where I could fill a hole in the market.

PRO TIP: Look for trends that have a high search rank but a low competition rank. Remember that Etsy is extremely competitive. You must seek out underserved markets to attract buyers. Avoid niches with a high competition rank or find a way to niche it down. The wedding niche is huge on Etsy and the competition is fierce. How can you niche down? What themes aren't being represented? What products aren't being offered? Those are the designs and items you'll want to focus on.

Note that you will see trademarked results show up on all these Etsy research tools, including eRank. For example, Taylor Swift, Harry Potter, and Star Wars all appear high on the list of trending products. Remember, however, that these are licensed brands that you cannot use. Yes, other sellers may be selling these trademarked products now, but it's only a matter of time before their listings are pulled. Don't risk your business by trying to sell licensed designs.

Etsycheck.com: Etsy Check is another tool that allows you to see the sales history and search ranking of specific products on Etsy. Its interface is simpler than eRank's but you don't get the in-depth data that eRank provides, especially when it comes to researching trends. I use Etsy Check to find keywords, specifically for use in tags, for my Etsy shop.

When I am creating an Etsy listing, I will log into Etsy Check, use the tag generator, and search for the item I am listing. For example, if I am listing a Christmas tote bag, I will type "Christmas tote bag" into the search bar. As with eRank, the results will show the competition for a particular keyword. For example, "Christmas bag" has the highest level of competition. However, "Xmas bag" has a much lower level of competition. This data would tell me that I should add "Xmas bag" to my title and tags. It would also encourage me to create bags that say "Xmas" rather than "Christmas."

Everbee.io: Like eRank and Etsy Check, Everbee is a tool that enables you to explore and study products on Etsy to uncover trends and opportunities within particular niches. With Everbee, you can find successful products in a given niche and gain inspiration for new offerings. Everbee, similar to eRank, offers a valuable resource for researching trends. Most Etsy sellers utilize either eRank or

Everbee, not both. Both platforms offer a free trial period for you to test before deciding whether to subscribe to a paid plan.

My Method: I use eRank for market research and Etsy Check for generating tags and keywords. It's important to keep in mind that these tools are not endorsed by Etsy and may not always provide accurate information. I use them as a reference rather than a definite source. Ultimately, the sales performance of my products is the true measure of their success.

I started my Etsy POD shop knowing that I wanted to sell vintage and retro-inspired products that coordinated with my Etsy sticker and magnet shop. I didn't start to use paid tools until several months into selling on Etsy. These paid tools can offer some help if you have no idea where to start researching trends or finding keywords and tags.

Selecting Products: After identifying your niche, focus on selling a single product first. This will help you understand what designs sell well and allow you to gradually expand your product offerings as you gain more knowledge of the POD market. My biggest mistake when I started my POD journey was trying to sell several assorted products. I had tee shirts, mouse pads, tote bags, and pet feeding mats in my shop. I was spreading myself so thin trying to manage all of the different product types that none were able to gain traction. By pulling back on focusing on just one product, I was better able to attract customers and grow my business.

Printify and Printful offer a lot of different products and it can be hard to select just one to start with. That being said, the most popular POD products sold on Etsy are:

Tee Shirts: Almost everyone wears tee shirts, so it's no surprise they are one of the most popular products in the print-on-demand industry. They are versatile items that can be printed with a wide range of designs, from plain text to complex graphics. They are also an affordable option for both the seller and the customer as they cost less than full-sleeved tops, pants, or jackets.

T-shirts can be made from a variety of materials, including cotton, polyester, and a blend of both. It's important to note materials when choosing tee shirts as you'll want to include fabric details in your Etsy listings. Tee shirts come in numerous assorted styles, such as short-sleeve, long-sleeve, tank tops, v-neck, and crewneck. Sizes include men's, women's, unisex, and children's.

Hoodies & Sweatshirts: Hoodies and sweatshirts are popular print-on-demand products because they offer comfort, warmth, and the ability to be printed with a wide range of designs, making them suitable for a variety of uses. They are of course most popular in the colder months, and many shoppers buy them to give as holiday gifts.

Hoodies and sweatshirts are typically made from a blend of cotton and polyester, making them soft, warm, and durable. Just as with tee shirts, be sure to note the fabric content of any hoodies or sweatshirts you list on Etsy as some customers are particular about those details. Both hoodies and sweatshirts are available in unique styles, such as pullovers, zip-ups, and crewnecks, offering customers a range of options to choose from. Like t-shirts, hoodies, and sweatshirts can be printed in varied sizes and colors, allowing for further customization.

PRO TIP: While it's common to offer assorted sizes of tee shirts, hoodies, or sweatshirts within the same listing, it can be advantageous to separate your listings by gender. For example, creating a listing for women's sizes and a separate listing for men's sizes. While many of the shirts offered by the POD print providers are unisex, they also offer men's and women's specific sizes and cuts; and many Etsy shoppers search by gender.

Phone Cases: Phone cases are a popular print-on-demand product because they offer a way for customers to personalize and protect their devices. Shoppers turn to Etsy to find phone cases that aren't available in stores, so you'll need to be creative to create designs that will sell. A trip to any big box store to look at the cell phone case aisle will give you inspiration into what designs you might create that aren't being offered.

Phone cases can be printed with a wide range of designs, including photos, text, graphics, and prints, making them a popular choice for personal use or as gifts. Phone cases are typically made from plastic or silicone material, protecting them from scratches and minor impacts. They are available for a variety of phone models, including the latest iPhone and Android devices, ensuring a good fit for the customer's device.

Print-on-demand phone cases offer an elevated level of customization, allowing customers to choose the size, color, and design of their cases. Offering a variety of sizes can attract a wider range of customers who use different phone models, but it also involves keeping a larger number of listings up.

PRO TIP: If you decide to open a phone case POD shop where the only items you sell are phone cases, you might consider creating one listing for each phone model. For example, Printify offers several assorted styles of phone cases, and each style is available in multiple iPhone sizes. You can create one listing for each of your designs with the multiple phone options available, or you could create separate listings for each model. Separate listings would allow you to maximize the keywords and tags within each listing to specify the specific model, which would help your listing be found for customers searching for their phone's specifications.

Tote Bags: Tote bags are a popular print-on-demand product because of their versatility and practicality. They can be used for a wide range of purposes, such as shopping, carrying books, or carrying personal items. Tote bags are used for school, work, and travel by all ages and genders. They are also a popular choice for businesses looking to promote their brand, as they can be custom printed with a logo or design.

Tote bags are typically made from cotton or canvas material, making them durable and long-lasting. On Etsy, you will note that most tote bags are listed as "canvas." These bags come in assorted sizes, colors, and styles, allowing for customization to suit the customer's needs. Special occasion and holiday tote bags are popular as are "farmer's market tote bags" and "book bags."

Note that most tote bags come in various sizes. For example, the tote bags on Printify come in three sizes. You can choose to only offer one size to make it less confusing for customers. Or if you choose to offer all three sizes, you could create three separate listings for small, medium, and large. I find it easier to select one size of tote bag that fits with the niche you are targeting. For example, the 12x12-inch size tote bag is the perfect size for a book bag while the 14x14-inch size is better suited as an overnight bag.

Posters & Prints: If you are an artist who creates your own designs, consider putting your artwork onto posters and prints and selling them via an Etsy POD shop. Posters are typically made of paper, while canvas prints are on a piece of canvas that is stretched on a wood frame.

Coffee Mugs: Coffee mugs are a popular print-on-demand product because they are affordable and practical while also allowing users to choose designs based on their personal style and interests. Coffee mugs also make great gifts for any occasion or holiday.

The various POD providers offer a wide variety of sizes and colors of coffee mugs, as well as design options. You can create your own designs or offer to have mugs customized with names, dates, and even photos. Personalized coffee mugs are especially popular for events such as retirement parties and weddings.

Stickers: Stickers, particularly sticker sheets of personalized stickers, are a popular print-on-demand product because of their versatility and affordability for both the customer and seller. Offering stickers via a POD provider means you as the seller do not have to keep an inventory of stickers on hand. This allows you to offer more designs as well as personalization options.

There are two main camps when it comes to stickers: sticker sheets and single stickers. While selling single stickers via a POD service is typically too costly for customers (the cost of a single sticker plus shipping can be as much as $10), sticker sheets can be a good fit for a POD business model. The POD providers offer various sizes of sticker sheets that you can either sell with ready-made designs or that you can customize based on buyer requests.

PRO TIP: When choosing products on Printify, I first look at the current best-selling products on the site, which they have listed in a dedicated section. I then look at the ratings for each product, choosing the one with the best ranking. I then make sure that the product is printed and shipped within the same country as my shop to ensure customers receive their orders as quickly as possible. And before making my final decision, I take a good look at the product cost and shipping charge to ensure it is a product that is affordable for buyers. Sometimes I will find a fantastic product, but the shipping cost is so high that it is unreasonable to expect that customers will pay.

Finding a best-selling product with a high ranking that is printed and shipped within the country of your shop and that is priced fairly will give you the best chance of making sales on Etsy.

Expanding Your Product Line: While I recommend starting with just one product in your Etsy shop, as time goes on, you may want to add other products that compliment your main product offering.

For instance, you could start with holiday-themed coffee mugs as your first product, as these are popular gifts during the Christmas season. After the holiday is over, you can look at your sales and pick out the best-selling designs. You could then expand your offerings to include other products with the same designs, including such items as holiday cards, ornaments, or even festive tee shirts. The hope is that customers will see your best-selling coffee mug designs and then be inspired to add to their orders other products with those same designs.

It's important to keep testing and refining your product offerings to see what resonates best with your target audience and what is selling. If you started your shop selling tote bags, you could eventually add accessory makeup bags to your store. If you started selling women's tee shirts, you could expand to matching children's shirts, which fall under the "mommy and me" aesthetic.

And if you find a product that just isn't selling? Then you can delete it and find a new product to try. If the potholders you thought would sell well aren't, but you want to stick with kitchen accessories, try aprons or tea towels. If you find that you can't break through the competition with the sweatshirts you have been designing, switch to clothing that most stores aren't offering, such as leggings or dresses.

The beauty of POD is that you aren't ever stuck with a product or design. You aren't having to order and store inventory the way a traditional retail store does. If you create a design that isn't selling, delete it. If you decide you don't want to offer a specific product, delete it.

Personalization: There are two main types of print-on-demand shops: those that sell pre-designed products and those that offer customization. All the information we've discussed so far is relevant for selling pre-designed products where each customer will receive the same item that is pictured in the listing. The thumbnail for the coffee mug listed is the coffee mug they will receive.

But there's another size of POD, and that's personalized products, also called customized products. This means that customers can have you add their own text, images, or designs to the product, resulting in a unique, one-of-a-kind item. This type of POD involves additional steps, such as setting up customization options within your Etsy listings and handling the creation and proofing process through your POD provider. However, this business model allows you to charge more for your products, meaning you will make more money. And it isn't as competitive as most Etsy POD shops do not offer personalization.

Popular personalized POD items include things like:

- **Customized tee shirts and sweatshirts:** These are especially popular for family vacations and reunions as well as bachelor and bachelorette parties. Businesses also order personalized shirts for staff and clients.
- **Personalized phone cases:** Personalized phone cases are popular with individuals who want to add an individualized touch to their device, such as adding a favorite photo or design, a monogram, or a special message. They are also unique and thoughtful gifts for someone else, especially around the holidays. Additionally, businesses and organizations may use personalized phone cases as promotional items to showcase their brand.

- **Customized mugs:** Think of coffeemugs for couples that are printed with their names and a special date; photo mugs for families and even pets; monogrammed mugs with initials or a full name; mugs as party favors with the date of the event; and mugs celebrating someone's achievements such as graduating high school or starting a new job.
- **Personalized tote bags:** Custom tote bags are especially popular in the bridal category. The bridal market is huge on Etsy, and brides are in search of customized bags for their bridesmaids and groomsmen. Putting names, initials, or monograms on bags is a popular shop model, as is creating tote bags with photos on them.
- **Customized jewelry:** Print-on-demand jewelryis a low-competition niche as few Etsy sellers offer it. Those that do sell custom jewelry are usually hand-making the pieces, and the prices are much higher than a POD piece. Customers are looking for jewelry with names, initials, and special dates engraved on them. And jewelry is a great gift for all occasions and holidays, meaning jewelry POD shops have a steady stream of sales year-round.
- **Personalized stickers:** Stickerswith images or text aren't just for businesses. Parents buy stickers customized with their children's names, and adults buy them to put on water bottles and laptops. And don't forget about those stickers that you see on the back of car windows with the family represented in stick figures with their names below each member. There are entire Etsy shops that sell nothing but personalized family car stickers.
- **Customized keychains:** Keychains printed with names or logos are not only popular with businesses but also for party favors, stocking stuffers, and giveaways.
- **Personalized hats**: Hats with embroidered text or logos can be ordered for various occasions, such as a family reunion, a sports team, a company, a group of friends, or as a gift for someone special. People may want to add their name, a design, a logo, a message, or a picture to the hat. Personalized hats can also be a way to promote a brand or a cause.

- **Customized notebooks:** Notebooks printed with names, messages, or even photos can be ordered by customers for various purposes such as customs notebooks for specific classes, planners with personalized covers, journals with photos, or notebooks for drawing or sketching that are printed with custom names or initials. These notebooks can also make for great personalized gifts for friends, family, and co-workers, or special events and occasions like birthdays, anniversaries, or graduations.
- **Personalized mouse pads**: Also called "mouse mats," these computer accessories can be ordered with custom images, graphics, logos, or text. They make unique and affordable gifts for friends, family, or co-workers.
- **Pet products:** Pet owners often personalize products for their pets, such as custom-printed collars, leashes, bandanas, clothing items like tee shirts or hoodies, and custom-printed pet beds. They may include their pet's name, image, or design that represents their personality or breed. Personalized pet products are popular as gifts for pet owners.
- **Baby clothes:** Baby clothes can be personalized with names, birth dates, initials, or unique designs related to the baby's interests or hobbies. Personalized baby clothes make great gifts for baby showers, birthdays, and holidays.

While a POD shop that offers personalization is a strong business model, there are pros and cons to offering customers the opportunity to customize their products.

Pros of customization:

1. **Increased customer engagement and loyalty.** If a customer is happy with your customized products, they will likely return to your shop to create more personalized products for themselves and to give them as gifts. Since many customized products are for group events such as weddings, reunions, and vacations, you have a better chance of repeat buyers who come back to you for their yearly customized shirts or bags.

2. **Unique and customizable products that stand out from competitors.** Since fewer Etsy POD shop owners offer customizable products, you will have a leg up on the competition. And the more customization that you offer, the better chance you have of attracting buyers. For example, most shops that offer customization only offer text. But if you offer photo customization, you will have an advantage in the marketplace.
3. **Potential for higher profit margins on personalized items.** Because of the extra work of personalizing designs before an item is sent to production and due to the unique nature of the final product, sellers can usually charge more for personalization. If you have even been on a website that offers customization – say, monogrammed initials on towels or embroidered Christmas stockings with your children's names on them – you have seen the cost of personalizing those products.
4. **Ability to target specific market niches.** Offering to customize products for specific holidays and events helps to differentiate your shop from the rest, leading to multiple quantity orders and repeat business. Whether it's selling personalized wedding weekend tote bags or customized tee shirts for all the teachers in a school, the more customization options you offer, the more you will stand out from the competition and attract more business.

Cons of customization:

1. **Slower production times and increased workload.** If you offer customization, you will need to modify your Etsy listings with space for customers to enter their personalization requests. You will also need to create more mockups showing the numerous ways your products can be customized. And since you will need time to create these custom designs, the production times for your products will take longer, meaning customers will wait longer for their orders.
2. **Possible need for additional software or equipment.** Depending on the types of personalization and product

customization you are offering, you may need to invest in better graphic software and a more powerful computer system to handle more complex designs. Selling shirts customized with photos, for example, means you will need high-resolution pictures, which you also may need to edit.

3. **Difficulty in managing customer expectations and requests.** When you are creating a product where the design will differ from the one shown in the listing, it can lead to customer confusion, especially if fonts and colors don't come out exactly as the buyer expects. Customers may also want more customization than you are offering. For example, you may offer coffee mugs printed with two lines of custom text. But a customer might expect you to create a design with an entire paragraph of text as well as a photo.
4. **Risk of receiving negative reviews or returns from dissatisfied customers.** Personalized products run the biggest risk of having unhappy customers who don't like the way the product turned out or are angry that the item took so long to arrive. Or they could have made a mistake on their end – for example, misspelling a name or giving you the wrong date – that they don't see until they receive the product, causing them to demand a refund, even though they were at fault.

A Hard Truth: By now you are likely excited about starting your Etsy POD shop. You've thought about and researched different niches and have settled on one. And you have selected your print provider and chosen your first product to start putting designs on. You are likely really excited about the opportunity, confident in your choices, and positive that customers will start ordering your items immediately.

But you are about to be in for a wakeup call as the vast majority of the products you list on Etsy will not sell. In fact, it's common in the industry for POD shops to make the majority of their sales on only 20% of their items, with the other 80% never selling.

Let me repeat that: **80% of the POD products you list on Etsy will never sell.**

This is the reality of the POD industry, and it is important to be prepared for it. The key is to continually evaluate your shop and products, experimenting with different designs and products until you find what resonates with your target audience. The more you experiment, the better your chances are of finding the products that will sell. Don't give up and keep trying different strategies until you find what works best for your shop.

The good part of this is that since the up-front costs to run a POD shop are so low, it won't break the bank to test many distinct products and designs. You can experiment with different ideas, designs, and products until you find what sells. With low overhead costs and the ability to quickly change your product offerings, POD provides a low-risk platform for starting an online business and testing your creative ideas.

And while it can hurt when a product you put a lot of work into creating doesn't sell, you need to train yourself to focus on the products that do. POD is all about making sales. If you want to create art for the sake of art, you would be better off painting or hand-making jewelry. With POD, your focus is on finding profitable niches and listing numerous products until you find the handful that sells. And it's that 20% that can earn you a full-time income. It's the 20% that will eventually become your focus. However, you need the 80% to get there.

It's important to keep in mind that success in the POD business does not happen overnight, and it may take time for your products to gain traction and start selling. But by giving each listing a full year, you allow enough time for it to potentially perform well and make the effort worth it. If a product isn't selling after a year, it's okay to let it go and focus on the ones that are performing well, as it can help you streamline your product offerings and focus on what's working.

As you continue your POD journey, you will eventually find your perfect niche and perfect product offering. You will learn about what customers want and increase your speed in creating those designs. Your processes will become faster, your confidence will increase, and your Etsy POD shop will grow!

CHAPTER FOUR: HOW TO CREATE PRINT-ON-DEMAND DESIGNS

So far, we've covered what you need to start an Etsy POD shop. We've gone over researching niches, choosing products, and choosing your print-on-demand provider. But before you can list POD items for sale on Etsy, you must create them. And to create products, you first need a design. After all, you aren't going to be able to sell plain white tee shirts. The shirts need to have a graphic on them!

There are several ways to create designs for your POD products:

- **Use graphic design software**
- **Hire a freelance designer**
- **Use pre-made templates**
- **Utilize design generators**

Using graphic design software: There are various graphic design software options available that can help you create designs for your Etsy POD products. Note that these specific programs require you to draw your graphics or combine elements such as vectors and text to create your unique designs. The most popular options for this include:

- **Adobe Illustrator** is a professional-grade vector graphics software that is commonly used in the design industry. It offers a wide range of tools and features that make it ideal for creating designs for POD products, such as t-shirts, mugs, and bags. Illustrator is a paid software program, but it provides a free trial so you can try it out before committing to a subscription.
- **Canva** is an online graphic design tool that is perfect for beginners and those with no design experience. It's an easy-to-use platform that provides a range of templates and design elements, so you can quickly create eye-catching designs for your products. Canva is a great option for Etsy POD sellers as it allows you to create designs for a wide range of products, including t-shirts, posters, and social media graphics.
- **Inkscape** is a free and open-source vector graphics software that provides similar features to Illustrator. It's ideal for those who are on a budget and prefer not to pay for software. Inkscape is a great option for those who are new to graphic design as it has a learning curve that is easier to navigate than Illustrator.

Hire a freelance designer: Most of us are not graphic designers, and that's okay! When it comes to starting an Etsy POD shop, the truth is that most sellers are not designing their products. One option some use is to hire a designer to make graphics for them.

A freelance designer is an independent contractor who offers design services to clients on a project basis. When you hire a freelance designer, you can choose someone who specializes in the specific design style you're looking for or someone who has experience creating designs for similar projects.

There are several places where you can find freelance designers to hire to create POD graphics:

- **Freelance websites:** Websites such as **Upwork**, **Freelancer**, and **Fiverr** are all great places to find and hire freelance designers. These sites allow you to browse the portfolios of many different designers, compare their rates and skills, and select the best fit for your project. You can also post jobs for designers to apply for.

- **Social Media:** You can also search for freelance designers on social media platforms such as **LinkedIn**, **Facebook**, and **Instagram**. Many designers have profiles on these platforms that showcase their work and contact information. Search the hashtag #graphicdesigner to find results.
- **Design Communities:** Design communities such as **Dribble,Behance**, and **AIGA** are great places to connect with designers and find inspiration. You can also reach out to designers you admire and see if they are available for hire.
- **Direct Outreach:** If you know a designer you would like to work with, reach out to them directly. This could be a former coworker, someone you met at a conference, or someone you know through a mutual friend. You can also use your social media accounts to ask friends and family if they know of any graphic designers.

If you decide to hire a freelance designer, you'll need to communicate your vision and requirements clearly to ensure you get the design you want. You can provide the designer with examples of other designs that you like, as well as any specific colors or styles you want them to use. It's important to be clear about the budget for the project and any deadlines that need to be met. Since you need a lot of graphics for a POD business, it's best if you can find someone who will deliver batches of designs, not just one.

One of the benefits of hiring a freelance designer is that you have complete control over the final design. You can request changes or revisions until you are completely satisfied with the result. Freelance designers are typically able to work quickly and deliver high-quality designs.

However, good graphic designers aren't cheap. While you may get great graphics, there's no guarantee that they will end up selling. It can be risky to invest money when you aren't sure of the payout. And you want to make sure that the designer isn't selling the same artwork to anyone else.

Use pre-made templates: Hiring a freelance designer can be a great option to create designs, but it can also be costly. A more affordable option is to purchase pre-made templates, which refer to pre-designed graphics or designs that can be purchased and used as is or modified for a specific purpose.

In the context of an Etsy POD shop, pre-made templates refer to designs that have already been created and are available for purchase. These templates can be used on POD products such as t-shirts, mugs, and bags, among others, without having to create designs from scratch or hire someone to make them.

The advantages of using pre-made templates include:

- **Timesaving:** As the designs have already been created, you do not have to spend time coming up with the initial design.
- **Cost-effective:** Hiring a graphic designer can be expensive, but using pre-made templates is a more cost-effective alternative.
- **Versatility:** Pre-made templates come in a variety of styles and themes, making it easy to find one that fits your specific needs.
- **Easy customization:** Most pre-made templates can be easily customized with your own added text. Or you can alter the color in a program such as Canva.

Pre-made templates can be purchased from various websites and marketplaces, such as **Creative Market**, **Envato Elements,** and **Graphic River,** to name a few. These websites offer a range of templates for different purposes, including graphic design, web design, print design, etc. You can browse their collections, preview the templates, and purchase the images that you want for your POD products. Additionally, many print-on-demand providers offer pre-made design templates that you can customize and use for your products right in your POD account.

Creative Fabrica is by far the most popular website for pre-made templates to use in Etsy POD shops. Creative Fabrica is a digital marketplace for graphic design resources such as fonts, graphics, and pre-made templates. It's a popular destination for Etsy POD shop owners because it offers a vast selection of resources for a variety of design needs. On the site, you can browse through a collection of pre-made templates, which can be used as a starting point for your designs. These templates can be edited and customized to suit your needs and style. The site offers a wide range of templates, including those for t-shirts, mugs, and other products.

In addition to pre-made templates, Creative Fabrica also offers a wide selection of graphics and fonts, which can be used to create your designs. The graphics come in a variety of styles and themes, including nature, holidays, and abstract patterns. The fonts section offers a variety of hand-written, script, and sans-serif styles that can be used to add text to your designs.

Creative Fabrica offers a subscription-based model, with plans starting at $9.95 per month. With a subscription, you have access to all of the templates, graphics, and fonts on the site. The subscription also includes new resources added to the site each week from different designers across the globe.

PRO TIP: When using Creative Fabrica, you need to make sure that the graphics you choose have a **print-on-demand license**, not just a commercial license. The print-on-demand license specifically allows you to use graphics to create products that you can sell through print-on-demand services like Etsy POD. If you only have a commercial license, you may be limited in how you can use the graphics and could potentially face legal issues if you use them in an unauthorized way. You can select the “Print On Demand” option when searching the site so that only those images suitable for POD are shown to you.

BONUS TIP: When exploring the graphics on Creative Fabrica, **prioritize sorting by new images**. Since Creative Fabrica is heavily used by Etsy POD sellers, the most frequently used designs tend to be listed first, meaning they've already been acquired by numerous other sellers. By prioritizing new images, you'll have the first opportunity to use the newest offerings on the site that haven't been sold on Etsy yet.

Utilize design generators: Design generators are online tools that allow you to create designs for your products without any design experience. These tools often feature pre-made templates and graphics, along with a user-friendly interface that makes it simple to customize your designs. Some popular design generators include **Canva**, **Placeit**, and **PicMonkey**.

With a design generator, you can choose a template, upload your graphics or photos, add text, and make other modifications to create a unique design. The key to success with design generators is to understand how to use the software and how to make effective use of the graphics and templates that are available. Design generators are a great option for Etsy POD sellers who want to create their designs without having to learn graphic design skills or hire a freelance designer.

PRO TIP: Most Etsy POD shops that use pre-made graphics from sites such as **Creative Fabrica** also use **Canva** to edit the images before uploading them to a site such as Printify to be placed onto products. Note that you will want to upgrade to a Canva Pro subscription to use their images and graphics legally for POD.

The process of editing images in Canva is simple:

1. Once you've found a design you like on Creative Fabrica, download it in the file format you need. The most common file formats for POD products are PNG and JPG.
2. After downloading the file, open it in Canva and start editing. Canva has a user-friendly interface that makes it easy to customize designs, even if you don't have any graphic design experience. You can change the color, add text, or adjust the size of the design to fit the product.
3. Once you're happy with the design, download it to your computer in the desired format and then upload it to your print provider's website. From there, you can add it to the product and start selling it on your Etsy shop.

Customizing images from Creative Fabrica in Canva can be done in several ways. You can change the size, orientation, and aspect ratio of the image. You can also adjust the color palette, brightness, contrast, and saturation. You can add filters, masks, and overlays to further change the look of the image. Additionally, you can add elements such as shapes, lines, and illustrations to the design.

Adding text in Canva is a straightforward process. You can choose from a variety of pre-made text templates, or you can create your own by adding text boxes and customizing the font, size, color, and alignment. You can also add drop shadows, outlines, and effects to make the text stand out. With Canva's drag-and-drop interface, you can easily position the text where you want it on the image.

Again, note that you will want to pay for a **Canva PRO** subscription if you plan to use any of their fonts or graphics in your designs. Otherwise, you could face copyright infringement if you use any of their elements in a design that you sell.

If you are a visual learner, note that numerous YouTube videos offer Canva tutorials, including those for creating Etsy POD products. Two channels I recommend are "Heather Studio" and "Cassiy Johnson," both of which offer step-by-step tutorial videos for creating graphics using Creative Fabrica, Canva, and Printify.

MY PROCESS: Here are the steps I take to create an image for a POD product:

1. I search Creative Fabrica for images I want by typing in a keyword or two into the search bar.
2. I sort the results by "newest first" to ensure I'm seeing graphics that few if any other sellers are using.
3. I select the "print on demand" license on the left side of the page to make sure I'm only seeing images that are licensed to be put onto physical products to sell.
4. I scroll through the images, clicking on the ones that interest me most and selecting "Add To Favorites," which will place them in a separate area for me to access easily.
5. I avoid graphics that have been downloaded by too many other sellers as that means it's likely already being used on numerous POD products.
6. I download the image I want to my computer. Most images are downloaded in a ZIP file. I open the ZIP file and move the image I want (jpg) to a folder on my desktop.

7. I open Canva Pro and click on “Create a design. ..
custom size 4x4-inch blank image.
8. I click on “Upload” and select the image I downloaded from Creative Fabrica.
9. I add the image to my 4x4-inch blank graphic and play around with colors. I also may add text or elements from the Canva Pro options.
10. Once I’m happy with how the image looks, I save it to my computer.
11. I save the image to my computer as a png file.
12. I log in to my POD print provider and upload the image to my account.
13. I choose a product to place the image on, centering it using the tools provided.
14. I save the design as a draft for later to list on Etsy.

Whether you draw your graphics, hire a designer, pay for images, use design generators, or do a mix of two or more, don’t let the fear of creating images stand in the way of launching your Etsy POD shop. Some of the most successful print-on-demand business owners have zero design experience. However, by researching niches and seeking out design resources, they have been able to build full-time print-on-demand businesses. And if they can do it, so can you!

APTER FIVE: ING YOUR ETSY SHOP

By now you understand what POD is, the various print providers available, how to research niches, how to narrow down your product offerings, and how to create graphics. But before you can start selling on Etsy, you first need to open an Etsy shop!

The first step in becoming an Etsy seller is to create a seller account. If you already have an account as an Etsy shopper, you will need to provide additional information for approval to sell on the platform, not just make purchases.

To set up an Etsy seller account, you will need to follow these steps:

1. Go to the **Etsy website** and click on the **Sell on Etsy** button.
2. Click the **Open your Etsy shop** button.
3. Enter your email address and password to create an account or sign in with an existing account.
4. Choose your shop language, country, and currency.
5. Select a **shop name** that represents your brand and is memorable to customers.
6. Agree to Etsy's terms of use and policies.
7. Click the **Create your shop** button to complete the process.

8. After setting up your account, you will need to add products and set up payment methods before you can start selling on Etsy.

Let's dig deeper into completing the process of opening an Etsy shop. To complete the process of setting up an Etsy seller account, you will need to **Create Your Etsy Shop** and configure your **Shop Preferences.** This can be done through the **Shop Manager**, accessible through the store-shaped icon in your Etsy **Seller Dashboard.** It is possible to skip this step and return later to set up your store, or to modify your settings at any time in the future.

PRO TIP: I have my **Shop Manager** bookmarked on my desktop computer so that I can quickly access it to create new listings and process orders. I also have the **Etsy Seller App** installed on my phone so I can easily access my account from anywhere at any time.

Etsy Shop Preferences are settings that allow you to customize and manage various aspects of your Etsy shop. You can access your shop preferences by going to **Shop Manager** and clicking on the **Preferences** tab.

Here are some of the things you can do in your **Etsy Shop Preferences**:

- Set your shop location and language.
- Set your shop policies, such as your return policy and shipping policies.
- Customize your shop's appearance by adding a banner image, logo, and other branding elements.
- Set your payment methods and choose which currencies you want to accept.
- Enable automatic renewal for your listings.
- Choose how you want to handle orders, including setting up automatic email responses.
- Set up Google Analytics to track your shop's performance.
- Set up shipping profiles to streamline the process of shipping your products.
- Enable or disable various features, such as the ability to offer gift wrapping or to allow customers to request custom orders.

Time Commitment: When setting up your Etsy shop, you will be asked about your **Time Commitment**, which refers to your level of dedication as a seller. This information is solely for Etsy's informational purposes and will not impact your eligibility to sell on the platform or have any effect on your shop or account. You have the option to select whether selling on Etsy is your full-time or part-time job, or you can leave the question unanswered, it is completely your choice.

Shop Name: It's crucial to choose an appropriate shop name for your branding on Etsy. Your shop name should reflect your brand and be easy for customers to remember and spell. If you have a specific niche and know the type of products you'll offer, choose a name that aligns with that. However, avoid a name that's too narrow, as it might restrict you from expanding your product line as your shop grows. For example, naming your shop "Bridesmaids Apparel" will limit you if you decide to offer items other than clothing – say, coffee mugs or water bottles - in the future. However, "Beautiful Bridesmaids" implies your niche while allowing room for growth.

Note that while you have the option to change your shop name later, try to choose a name that you intend to keep from the start. This is because switching your shop name can cause confusion for your customers and may necessitate updates to your branding elements and promotional campaigns, including changing all of your social media handles.

It's also important to note that your shop name must adhere to Etsy's naming guidelines and cannot contain any prohibited words or phrases. Etsy has certain requirements and guidelines for shop names to ensure that they are appropriate and do not violate the platform's policies. Here are some of the main requirements and guidelines for shop names on Etsy:

- Shop names must be unique and not already in use by another Etsy seller.
- Shop names must not contain any prohibited words or phrases, such as offensive language or trademarked terms.

- Shop names must not imply that you are affiliated with Etsy or any other company or organization.
- Shop names must not contain any personal information, such as phone numbers or addresses.
- Shop names must not be too long or difficult to spell or pronounce.

- Shop names must be 4-20 characters in length.
- Shop names cannot contain spaces or special characters.
- Shop names cannot contain profanity.
- Shop names are exclusive to one shop, meaning you can't create a shop name that is already being used by an existing Etsy member.
- Shop names cannot infringe on another's trademark.

Set Up Payment & Billing: In the next step of setting up your Etsy shop, you will be required to provide payment and billing information. This includes entering a valid payment method that Etsy can use to charge you in case your fees exceed your sales. Remember that when you sell a POD item, Etsy will automatically take out their fees and shipping costs, depositing the remaining balance in your Etsy account. If you have to process a refund, your Etsy balance might fall into the negative, meaning they will charge your credit card for any fees you've occurred.

You also need to specify a method for Etsy to pay you for your sales. You can choose to have your money deposited daily, once a week, once every two weeks, or once a month. As your POD shop grows, you will want to schedule daily payments to pay the credit card your print provider is charging your product and shipping costs. Large Etsy POD shops need to keep on top of these charges to avoid maxing out their credit cards, which would result in orders not going through.

To set up your Etsy shop's payment and billing, you will need to follow these steps:

1. Go to the **Shop Manager** and click on the **Finances** tab.
2. Click on the **Payment settings** option.

3. Since your orders will be processed through Etsy, they choose the payment methods they accept.
4. Click the **Save** button to save your payment settings.

When setting up your Etsy seller account, you will need to provide different information based on whether you are registering as an individual/sole proprietorship or a business. If you're an individual/sole proprietor, you'll need to supply personal information like your name and contact information and, if an American, your social security number. If you're registering a business, you'll need to provide more details about your business, such as its official name, contact information, and any necessary documentation.

Confused about the difference between a sole proprietorship and an LLC? Don’t worry, most people are. And many people starting businesses are unsure about which is best for their new business.

A **sole proprietorship** is a business structure in which an individual owns and operates the business completely by themselves. The owner is responsible for all aspects of the business, including its debts and liabilities. In a sole proprietorship, the owner and the business are considered the same for tax purposes. In America, this means your social security number acts as your business ID when it comes to filing taxes.

On the other hand, a **limited liability company (LLC)** is a business structure that combines elements of both a sole proprietorship and a corporation. Like a sole proprietorship, an LLC is owned by an individual or group of individuals, but it offers its owners the liability protection of a corporation. This means that the owners of an LLC are not personally liable for the debts and obligations of the business.

Both sole proprietorships and LLCs have advantages and disadvantages, and the appropriate choice for your business will depend on your specific needs and circumstances. It is always a good idea to consult with a legal or financial professional before deciding on the best business structure for your company.

Most Etsy sellers, including myself, are sole proprietors. As explained above, being a sole proprietor simply means that I pay taxes as an individual, not a corporation, using my social security number and not a business license.

If you are an individual/sole proprietorship, this means that you are operating your Etsy shop as a one-person business and are not registered as a corporation or LLC with the government. As a sole proprietorship, you will pay taxes (in America) as an individual using your social security number and will not need a business license.

That's right: As a sole proprietor, you typically do not need to file any type of paperwork with your city, state, or federal governments for your Etsy shop; you will simply be taxed as an individual. Again, this is the case for most places in America; please check with a tax professional or lawyer in your area to see what the requirements are where you live.

If you are registering as an individual/sole proprietorship on Etsy, you will need to provide certain information on the **How you'll get paid** page during the setup process. This information may include:

- Your name and contact information.
- Your social security number or taxpayer identification number (TIN)
- Your bank account information, including the bank name, routing number, and account number.

Credit Card: Because you will be using Etsy's direct checkout to receive payments, you will need to provide your card information on the **How you'll get paid** page during the setup process. It is important to note that you must also provide your bank account information for Etsy to issue payouts to you. In addition, you will need to have a debit or credit card on file with Etsy in case your fees are more than your payouts. In this case, Etsy will charge the balance to your card. It is worth noting that if you sell more than you owe in fees, Etsy will simply deduct the fees from your payouts before issuing them to you.

Test Deposit: After you have entered your payment and billing information on Etsy, they may issue a small test deposit to your bank account or PayPal account to verify that the information was entered correctly. This is standard practice to ensure that your deposits are working properly and that you will be able to receive payouts from Etsy.

The test deposit is a small amount, less than a dollar, and you will not be required to pay it back. To complete the verification process, you will need to check your bank account or PayPal account to find the test deposit and confirm that it was received. Once you have found the test deposit, you can enter the amount on the **How you'll get paid** page to complete the verification process.

Note that the test deposit may take a few days to appear in your account, so be sure to check back periodically if you do not see it right away. If you have any issues with the verification process, you can contact Etsy's support team for assistance. You can easily contact Etsy support at any time and for any reason by following these steps:

1. Go to **www.etsy.com** and click the **Help & Policies** tab at the bottom of the page.
2. Scroll down to the **Contacting Etsy** section and click the **Contact Us** button.
3. Select the appropriate **category** for your issue from the dropdown menu.
4. Enter a **subject** and a **detailed description** of your issue in the provided fields.
5. Click the **Continue** button to submit your request.

Etsy support typically responds within 24 hours, although it can take longer during peak times.

Two-Factor Authentication: Two-factor authentication is an additional security measure that requires you to provide a verification code when signing in from an unrecognized browser or device. This helps to protect your account from unauthorized access and ensures that only you can access your Etsy shop.

To set up two-factor authentication, you will need to choose a method for receiving your verification code. Etsy allows you to receive your verification code in one of three ways:

1. **Text message:** If you choose this option, you will receive a text message with your verification code whenever you need to sign in from an unrecognized browser or device.
2. **Authenticator app:** If you choose this option, you will need to download an authenticator app on your phone and use it to generate your verification code whenever you need to sign in from an unrecognized browser or device.
3. **Email:** If you choose this option, you will receive an email with your verification code whenever you need to sign in from an unrecognized browser or device.

Set Up Your Storefront: Once you've gotten through entering your personal and banking information, verifying your account, and setting up two-factor authorization, you can move on to a more fun step, which is setting up your Etsy shop storefront!

To set up your Etsy shop storefront, follow these steps (note that we'll go over these options more in-depth later in this chapter):

1. Go to your Etsy seller dashboard and click the **Shop settings** tab.
2. Click the **Shop info & appearance** tab on the left side of the page.
3. Enter a **shop title** and **shop announcement** that will appear at the top of your shop's homepage.
4. Add a **shop banner** image that will appear at the top of your shop's homepage.
5. Add a **shop icon**, which is a small image that will represent your shop on Etsy.
6. Enter a **shop description** that will appear on your shop's homepage and in search results.
7. Click the **Save** button to save your changes.

Etsy Standard:*Etsy Standard* is the default shop level for all sellers on the platform. It provides essential features and functions needed to start selling on Etsy. This package includes the ability to create a seller account, which in turn creates an Etsy shop and lists items for sale.

Additionally, with *Etsy Standard*, sellers can customize their shop page to make it unique and attractive to potential buyers. The fee for this service is a listing fee of $0.20 per item, which is charged when a seller creates a new listing or relists an expired one. This fee is valid for a four-month period. With *Etsy Standard*, sellers have the basic tools they need to start and run a successful online shop.

To edit your Etsy Shop, first, log into your **Shop Manager**. Then **click on the pencil icon next to your shop's name**. This will bring up a page where you can edit your shop's banner, icon, and featured items area.

Etsy Plus:*Etsy Plus* is a premium service that offers advanced features and tools for sellers, beyond what is included in the basic *Etsy Standard* plan. For a **monthly fee of $10**, *Etsy Plus* members receive a budget of 15 credits for promoting their listings through the *Promoted Listings* and *Etsy Ads* programs, as well as an additional $5 for *Etsy Ads*.

Etsy Plus subscribers get advanced shop appearance options, a custom domain name, and access to Etsy's wholesale platform. In addition, *Etsy Plus* offers a discount on Hover domains, although sellers can choose to buy a domain from other providers such as GoDaddy. Note that a custom domain can greatly enhance the visibility and professionalism of a seller's Etsy shop and is a valuable tool for sellers looking to increase their online presence.

Featured Items: Featured items are listings or shop sections that are prominently displayed on a seller's shop page. All sellers on Etsy have the **Standard grid** option to feature up to four listings or shop sections on their shop page.

Etsy Plus subscribers have the additional option to use a **mixed grid layout.** With a mixed grid layout, *Etsy Plus* subscribers can feature one big listing or shop section along with four smaller items or shop sections on their shop page.

Note that you do not have to feature any items at the top of your store. However, if you do, be sure to carefully pick the items or sections you want to feature as they will be prominently displayed to customers and could impact their buying decisions. For example, if you selected Christmas items to be highlighted during the holiday season, don't forget to change them out after December 25th.

Discounts & Perks:*Etsy Plus* members enjoy exclusive savings and benefits that can boost their business and reduce costs. One of these benefits is a discount on marketing materials from **Moo**, a company specializing in exceptional printing and design services for businesses. With an *Etsy Plus* membership, you can save up to 30% on a range of materials from Moo, including business cards, flyers, and postcards.

Etsy Plus subscribers also benefit from a discounted rate on custom packaging from **BoxUp,** a company that provides customized packaging solutions for businesses. By taking advantage of the discount, *Etsy Plus* subscribers can save up to 20% on custom packaging from **BoxUp** and enhance the overall experience for their customers by presenting their products in a professional and branded manner. As a POD shop, you aren't going to be shipping your products, but as you grow, you might find yourself wanting some branded packaging for giveaways and public relations purposes.

Should you start your Etsy POD shop with *Etsy Standard* or upgrade to *Etsy Plus*? That is a choice only you can make. Most sellers start with *Etsy Standard* and then upgrade to *Etsy Plus* as their business grows. The listing and ad credits, the customization options, the advanced shop management, and promotional tools, and the priority customer support are, in my opinion, all well worth the $10 monthly fee.

Etsy Shop Icon: Your Etsy shop icon, also referred to as your logo or profile picture, is a small image that represents your shop on the Etsy platform. It appears next to your shop name on your shop's homepage, on your listings, and various other pages on the Etsy website and app. Ideally, you want to use this icon across all your social media platforms, making it the profile picture on every website your business is on.

To set up your **Etsy shop icon**, you will need to follow these steps:

1. Sign into your Etsy account and go to the **Shop Manager** section.
2. Click on **Settings** and then click on the **Info & Appearance** tab.
3. Scroll down to the **Shop Icon** section and click on the **Change Icon** button.
4. Select the image you want to use as your shop icon from your computer or device. The image must be at least 500 x 500 pixels and in a .jpg, .gif, or .png format.
5. Click on the **Save** button to apply your changes.

Shop Story: An **Etsy shop story** is where you can share a summary of your shop's products, values, and business philosophy. It is a chance for you to share your brand's story and connect with potential customers on a personal level. A well-written shop description can help to set your shop apart from others on the platform and make it more attractive to potential buyers.

To set up your **Etsy shop story** follow these steps:

1. Sign into your Etsy account and click on the **Shop Manager** button in the top right corner of the page.
2. Click on the **Settings** tab and then click on the **About Your Shop** tab.
3. Click on the **Story tab** at the top of the page.
4. Enter in a **Story Headline.**
5. Fill in the **Story** field.
6. You can also add a **Shop Video** here.
7. You can also add in **Shop Photos**.
8. You can also **add links to your social media pages**.
9. Click on the **Save** button to apply your changes.

Etsy Shop Title & Shop Announcement: The *Shop Title* and *Shop Announcement* are elements of your Etsy shop storefront that appear at the top of your shop's homepage. The *Shop Title* is a short, catchy phrase that represents your shop and its products. The *Shop Announcement* is a brief message that you can use to communicate essential information to your customers, such as new products or promotions.

The *Shop Title* and *Shop Announcement* are important because they can help to create a first impression on potential customers and set the tone for your shop. You should choose a *Shop Title* that accurately reflects the products and style of your shop and craft a *Shop Announcement* that is informative and engaging. Adding relevant keywords to your announcement is another effective way to maximize your Etsy SEO.

To access these areas, click on the **Settings** tab in your **Shop Manager** and then click on **Info & Appearance.** You can change these areas at any time or leave them blank until you are more comfortable filling them out.

Etsy Shop Banner: An Etsy shop banner is a large image that appears at the top of your shop's homepage and gives potential customers an idea of what your shop is all about. The banner image is an essential element of your shop's appearance, as it can help to create a professional and cohesive look for your shop and make a good first impression on potential customers. And while you don't have to have a banner, it's a terrific way to contribute to the branding of your business.

To edit your Etsy Banner, first, log into your **Shop Manager**. Then **click on the pencil icon next to your shop's name**. This will bring up a page where you can edit your shop's banner.

Make sure to choose a banner image that accurately reflects the products and style of your shop, and that is visually appealing and of the highest quality you can manage. You may want to consider hiring a professional graphic designer to create a banner image for you or use a design tool such as Canva to create a banner image on your own. Look at other Etsy shops to see what their banners look like to help you see how to best utilize this design element in your shop.

Mixed Grid: All Etsy shops have the option to use a *Standard Grid* but *Etsy Plus* shops can also choose a *Mixed Grid* option that features five listings or shop sections with a couple of layout choices.

To edit your grid options, first, log into your **Shop Manager**. Then **click on the pencil icon next to your shop's name**. This will bring up a page where you can edit your shop's **Featured Items** with your grid options.

I like to play around with the assorted options to see which works best for my shop. And I also periodically change out the images to keep my storefront looking fresh. Some of the top Etsy shops even change out their images daily so that frequent customers are always greeted with something new.

Hiring Out Design Services: You want to use consistent shop graphics across all of your social media platforms and in your promotional materials to create a cohesive brand image. If you can't design your logos and banners yourself, or you simply don't have the time to create them, you can hire graphic designers.

There are several places where you can hire a designer to create your Etsy shop logo, icons, and banners. Some options include:

1. **Fiverr:** Fiverr is an online marketplace where you can find freelance designers who offer a wide range of design services, including logo and banner design. You can browse through portfolios and reviews to find a designer who meets your needs and budget. It's easy to find a designer for under $10.
2. **Upwork:** Upwork is another online marketplace where you can find freelance designers for hire. You can post a job listing and receive proposals from designers who are interested in working with you. You will likely pay more for a designer on UpWork versus Fiverr, but the quality may also be better.
3. **99designs:** 99designs is a design contest platform where you can hold a design contest to receive multiple design options for your logo, icons, and banners. You can choose the design you like best and work with the designer to make any necessary revisions.
4. **Etsy:** You can also find designers on Etsy who offer design services, including logo and banner design.

Shop Options: You can find **Options** under the **Settings** tab in your shop managers. Etsy allows you to pre-determine several options for your store, including:

- **Rearrange Your Shop:** You can enable the feature to allow shop visitors to sort listings to their specifications. Or you can disable this feature so that the *Most Recently Listed* option is chosen.
- **Custom Order Requests:** If you are offering custom or personalized products, you can enable a setting where a *Request Custom Order* button will appear across your shop. If you do not offer personalized items, you will want to disable this feature. However, if you plan to offer custom POD products, you will need to enable this feature.
- **Offer Gift Wrapping & Gift Message:** You can enable or disable the option for buyers to add a message to the packing slip of their order. Because POD products are manufactured and shipped by a third-party, you won't be able to offer gift wrapping or gift messages.
- **Sold Listings:** You can choose to let other Etsy users see your sold listings, or you can hide them. Some sellers choose to hide their sold listings for fear that other sellers will see and then steal their best-selling designs. I let users see my sold listings so that customers can see my most popular items, which might help them decide to purchase them, too.
- **Current Time Zone:** You can set your shop's time zone here, which will help Etsy show customers an accurate delivery period. It takes packages longer to travel from California to New York than they do from within the same state.
- **Vacation Mode:** If you ever need to put your Etsy shop on vacation (whether because you are taking an actual vacation or are simply unable to process orders), you can easily put your entire store on vacation so that customers cannot purchase anything from your store. In fact, while your storefront will still be visible, your listings will be hidden. You can also include a *Vacation Announcement* that will display at the top of your shop. And you can write up a *Messages Autoreply*,

which will be sent to anyone who sends you a message while your *Vacation Mode* is on.

- **Close Shop:** Also under the *Options* section is a tab to close your Etsy shop. Note that if you have *Etsy Standard,* you only pay when you list an item. So, there is no reason to close your shop if you simply aren't listing new products. If you have an *Etsy Plus* account, you can simply cancel that subscription and leave your shop as is.

Shipping Policies: The shipping settings section of your Etsy account (accessible under the **Settings** tab) is where you can manage and configure the shipping options for your shop. Note that you can create shipping profiles within each of your listings to match up with the various products you are selling.

Note that when you have a POD shop, the print provider you use will have different shipping profiles depending on the products you sell. For example, if you use Printify, there will be a different shipping cost for a sweatshirt versus a coffee mug. If you plan to charge customers the shipping cost, you will simply let the print provider's setting integrate automatically into your Etsy shop. You will not have to create shipping profiles yourself.

PRO TIP: Most print-on-demand Etsy shops do not offer "free shipping," meaning they aren't building the cost of their shipping into the cost of the products. This is because the margins on POD products are already tight. And after Etsy fees, they are even slimmer. Shipping costs are constantly rising, making it difficult to add in those charges. And adding in the shipping costs just to offer "free shipping" can make the price of the item too expensive for many customers, especially when they can get the item for less from other shops.

Note that you can create different shipping profiles for distinct types of products or destinations and apply the shipping cost accordingly. You can also specify handling time for your products, which means how long it will take for your items to be shipped after an order is placed. This can help buyers to understand when they can expect to receive their orders. During the busy holiday season, it's common for sellers to adjust the processing and shipping times to account for the fact that the print providers are often running slower than usual.

We will cover shipping extensively later on in *Chapter Eight* of this book.

Policy Settings: Also, under the Settings section is where you can create your Policy Settings. Here you can set up the following:

- **Returns & Exchanges:** Etsy allows sellers to set their own policies for returns and exchanges on their products. These policies can vary from seller to seller, but generally include information on how to initiate a return or exchange, the period within which a return or exchange can be requested, and the conditions under which a return or exchange will be accepted. Some sellers may offer a full refund or exchange, while others may only offer store credit or a partial refund. Most POD Etsy shops do not offer returns or exchanges unless there was a problem with the product itself.
- **Cancellations:** The cancellations setting on Etsy allows sellers to set their policies for canceling orders. These policies can vary from seller to seller and can include information on the conditions under which a buyer can cancel an order and any fees that may be associated with the cancellation. With POD, it's important that you set clear cancellation policies because once you push an order through, it can't be stopped, meaning you will have to pay for it.
- **Privacy:** The privacy settings on Etsy allow users to control how their personal information is collected, used, and shared on the platform. These settings include options for controlling the types of information that is shared with Etsy and third-party partners, as well as options for managing communication preferences and account settings. In the privacy settings, users can choose to limit the types of information that Etsy collects from them, such as browsing data or search queries.
- **Fixed Polices**: The Fixed Policies section in an Etsy seller's dashboard is a set of pre-written policy templates that sellers can use to quickly create and publish their store policies, such

as their shipping, returns, and payment policies. These templates provide a basic framework for the seller to follow but can be customized to suit the specific needs of the seller and their business. As with returns and cancellations, be sure you are setting up clear policies and adjusting them during busy shopping seasons.

Production Partners: As a POD Etsy shop, you will always have at least one *Production Partner*, and that is the print provider you use. The print provider is usually automatically selected when you integrate them into your shop. For instance, if you are using Printify, Etsy will automatically add Printify as one of your *Production Partners.* And if you use any graphic design services, you will need to include those as well.

I have several *Production Partners* entered for my shop. Not only do I have them in the main *Production Partners* section, but I then choose which ones are specific for each listing. For example, if I purchased a graphic on Creative Fabrica and then had that graphic printed as a coffee mug through Printify, I would select both of those companies as the *Production Partners* when I listed that mug.

Not adding Production Partners can mean a designer could file a trademark infringement complaint on your listing, even if you purchased the graphic legally. Unfortunately, many Etsy shops steal artwork and try to pass it off as their own, meaning artists and designers have to keep their eyes on the site to see if someone is selling their work. Keeping up with entering any Production Partners you use will protect your shop and listings.

Community & Help: You can keep up with all of Etsy's announcements as well as get help under the *Community & Help* section, which is linked in your Shop Manager.

Facebook Shops: The *Facebook Shops* option in your Etsy seller dashboard allows you to connect your Etsy shop with your Facebook account and create a shop on Facebook. This allows you to sell your products directly on Facebook, in addition to your Etsy shop.

With *Facebook Shops*, you can create a personalized online store on Facebook, where you can highlight your products and make them available for purchase. You can also create posts and ads on Facebook to promote your products and drive traffic to your shop.

By connecting your Etsy shop to Facebook, you can easily import your products, product information, and inventory to your Facebook shop. This can save you time and effort as you do not have to manually upload your products to Facebook.

Once connected, you can also sync your inventory and sales across both platforms, so you don't have to worry about stock levels or order fulfillment between the two. Please note that you need to have a Facebook page set up before you can create a shop and connect it to your Etsy shop. Also, Facebook has certain policies and guidelines to follow regarding the use of its platform for commerce, make sure you are familiar with them before using *Facebook Shops*.

Etsy Fees: Now that you have your shop set up before you start integrating products from your POD provider, let's go over the fees that Etsy charges:

Listing Fees: Etsy charges a $.20 fee to list an item for sale on the platform. This fee is charged when a seller creates a new listing or relists an expired one. While no one likes to pay fees, the $.20 listing fee on Etsy is a reasonable cost, especially when compared to other popular e-commerce sites like Amazon or eBay. The Etsy listing fee covers a four-month listing period, and at the end of the four months, the seller can opt to renew the listing for another four months at the same cost of $0.20. So, the total cost for one item to be listed for a full year is only $0.80.

Transaction Fees: Etsy charges a transaction fee on each sale that is made through the platform. The 5% transaction fee on Etsy is a small price to pay for the exposure and resources provided by the platform. The fee is calculated on the sale price of each item, including shipping and gift-wrapping charges if there are any, and it helps cover the costs of running and maintaining the Etsy site.

Payment Processing Fees: Etsy partners with various payment processors to handle transactions on the platform, and these processors charge a fee for their services. This fee is typically around 2.9% + $.30 per transaction, which allows customers to pay for their orders using a variety of methods, including debit cards, credit cards, or PayPal. This service would cost sellers more if they set up payments directly, meaning the processing fees are quite affordable.

Shipping Label Fees: When a seller uses Etsy's shipping label feature, they are charged a fee that varies based on the shipping service and destination. The fee is calculated using the weight and dimensions of the package. This feature is a big advantage as Etsy seamlessly integrates with USPS to generate shipping labels, eliminating the need for manual input of customer addresses or calculation of postage costs. Upon receiving an order, Etsy automatically calculates the label fee based on the order weight and shipping destination. Sellers can then print the label out directly in their account, and the cost for the label is automatically deducted from their Etsy balance.

Despite criticism from sellers who don't like paying the fees, the fees charged by Etsy are necessary to support the platform's operations and upkeep. As individual sellers, the cost and time to set up and maintain a website with payment processing and shipping capabilities would be too much. Not to mention trying to get buyers to come to your site. Etsy has the traffic, customer base, and back-end systems that allow sellers to focus on selling, not website maintenance.

Advertising & Promotional Fees: In addition to the fees outlined above, Etsy offers various advertising and promotional options for sellers who want to increase the visibility of their products. These options come with additional fees, which vary depending on the specific advertising or promotion being used.

Etsy Ads: Etsy Ads is an advertising program that is available to sellers on a pay-per-click basis. This program allows sellers to advertise their products on Etsy directly on the site. Sellers set a daily budget and only incur charges when a customer clicks on their ad. This gives sellers control over their advertising expenses and the ability to adjust their budget as needed.

To access Etsy Ads, go to your **Seller Dashboard**, click on the **Marketing** tab, and select **Etsy Ads.**

Before investing in Etsy Ads, it is important to weigh the costs and benefits of the program. By setting a daily budget, sellers can control their advertising costs. A common starting point for many sellers is a $5 daily budget for one month, allowing them to assess the effectiveness of the ads before deciding to continue or make changes. Etsy Ads offers flexibility as sellers can start, stop, and adjust their budget at any time. The program is designed to increase product visibility and drive traffic to your shop, so if you aren't seeing results from your ads, it's easy to simply turn them off.

Etsy Offsite Ads: Etsy Offsite Ads provide sellers with an opportunity to reach a wider audience beyond the Etsy platform and beyond the scope of regular Etsy Ads. This can help to increase brand exposure and drive more sales for the seller as Etsy will be putting your products in front of shoppers on Google and other search engine sites.

To access Etsy Offsite Ads, go to your **Seller Dashboard**, click on the **Settings** tab, and select **Offsite Ads.**

It is important to carefully evaluate the costs and benefits of using Etsy Offsite Ads to determine if they are the right advertising strategy for your business, especially when you are first starting your shop. However, since you only pay for an ad when someone clicks on it AND then buys an item from your store, there is no reason not to use them.

If you sell less than $10,000 in a year on Etsy, Offsite Ads are an optional program you can opt into. However, Etsy Offsite Ads are mandatory for sellers who make over $10,000 in sales per year. But again, since sellers only pay when the ad results in a sale, there is no reason to be upset by being put into the program. After all, if you are selling over $10,000 in a year on Etsy, you are doing better than most other sellers. For me, mandatory Offsite ads are a sign of success!

Payment Processing: When I first started my online selling journey on eBay in 2005, accepting payments was a real hassle. PayPal was eBay's payment system, and many customers were wary of the site.

Some customers even sent me checks and cash through the mail to pay for their orders!

Today payment processing is built-in into all online selling sites, including Etsy. I don't have to worry about collecting money from my customers because Etsy takes care of all of that for me. Buyers can pay for their orders using various methods, including credit and debit cards, PayPal, and gift cards. Etsy takes care of the payment processing, holding the funds in escrow until the seller confirms the shipment of the order. This eliminates the need for sellers to send invoices or follow up on payments, as everything is automated through Etsy.

To take advantage of **Etsy Payments**, sellers must enroll in the service and connect a bank account to their Etsy account to get paid. When an order is placed through your shop, Etsy automatically processes the customer's payment. All fees and shipping costs are deducted from the total, and Etsy deposits the remaining funds into your Etsy account. The funds are then transferred to your bank account on the schedule you choose (daily, once a week, once every two weeks, or once a month).

Sales Tax: Selling on Etsy comes with a key advantage of the platform handling state sales tax collection and remittance on behalf of its sellers. This saves sellers a significant amount of time and effort as we don't have to collect and remit sales tax individually to each state, a requirement in most American states for online orders. This benefit of selling on Etsy is a major factor in why many sellers opt to keep their shop on the platform instead of setting up their own Shopify store. In fact, I have met successful Etsy POD shop owners who expanded to Shopify only to eventually go back to selling exclusively on Etsy for the sales tax collection alone!

Seller Protection: Etsy provides several protections for sellers on its platform, including:

Payment Protection: With Etsy Payments, buyers' funds are securely held until the order has been completed and the package has been delivered. When you print your shipping labels through Etsy, tracking is included, making it easy for packages to be tracked and delivery confirmed. This provides peace of mind for both buyers and sellers, as the buyer knows that their payment is secure and that their package is trackable, and the seller knows that they will receive payment for their products.

Dispute Resolution: Etsy's dispute resolution process is designed to help sellers and buyers resolve issues in a fair and timely manner. The process can involve either mediation, where Etsy acts as a mediator to facilitate communication between the parties, or arbitration, where Etsy makes a final decision on the dispute.

Both sellers and buyers can get help resolving any disputes through **Etsy's Help section.** Simply **scroll down to the bottom of any Etsy page** and locate the **Help** heading. Underneath, click on **Help Center.**

Seller Protection Insurance: Etsy offers seller protection insurance to eligible sellers in certain countries for orders under $250. Etsy may refund buyers and allow sellers to keep their earnings if a buyer never received their package because it was lost in transit, an item arrives damaged, or a buyer claims an item doesn't match the listing even though photos prove it does.

PRO TIP: If a buyer contacts you claiming an item hasn't been delivered but tracking shows it has, direct them to file a claim directly through Etsy. They can do this by clicking directly on their order and following the prompts on the screen. This removes you from the dispute process and puts the burden on Etsy directly to resolve the issue.

Shop Sections: A helpful feature you will want to utilize for your Etsy shop are the *Shop Sections,* which some refer to as *store categories*. Etsy *Shop Sections* are a way to organize your products into categories, making it easier for customers to navigate your shop and find the items they're looking for.

In a POD business, you can use *Shop Sections* to categorize your products by design, theme, product type, etc. This helps customers quickly find what they're interested in, and it helps you keep track of your inventory and manage your listings more efficiently. Plus, as you add additional products to your shop, dividing them into these sections can encourage customers to add on additional products.

To set up your Shop Sections, go to your **Seller Dashboard** and click on the **Listings** tab. On the right-hand side of the page will be the heading **Sections** with a drop-down menu underneath. Click on **Manage** to add and rearrange your shop categories. I personally like to arrange mine in alphabetical order.

As an example, if you're starting an Etsy shop selling women's tee shirts and have tops targeted to various professions, you can create sections based on the different careers. For example, you might create sections for teachers, nurses, lawyers, etc. On the other hand, if you have shirts for various holidays, you can create sections for Christmas, Valentine's Day, Easter, etc.

PRO TIP: One key aspect of Etsy is its search engine optimization or SEO. When you list an item, make sure to use the same keywords in the title, description, and tags. Additionally, aligning your shop sections with these categories can also help with SEO. For example, if you have tote bags specifically for use at farmer's markets, make sure "farmer's market tote bag" is included in the title, description, tags, and store section.

We'll cover SEO and listing your products on Etsy in the following chapters.

Linking Your POD Provider To Your Etsy Shop: Once your Etsy shop is set up, the next step is to integrate, or link, the print provider or providers you plan to use into your shop. Each of the print providers we've discussed earlier in this book will walk you step by step through the process of linking your Etsy shop to its system.

CHAPTER SIX: CREATING ETSY POD LISTINGS

Your Etsy shop setup is complete, with your chosen print provider linked to your account. You have also created designs, selected products, and created drafts in your print provider's account. It's now time for the last step: publishing the drafts on Etsy to make them available for customers to purchase!

In contrast to conventional Etsy listings made through the Seller Dashboard, print-on-demand requires activation in the dashboard of your chosen print provider. Although the user interface may vary slightly between print providers, the process of creating and publishing listings is generally similar across all platforms.

Since most new Etsy POD shops utilize Printify, we'll use it as the reference for explaining how to complete your drafts and publish them for sale on Etsy.

Let's say you have decided to focus on selling sweatshirts. You have chosen a unisex option on Printify and have started putting your design into drafts, which are saved in your Printify dashboard. When you are ready to finally list one of the sweatshirts for sale on Etsy, you will simply open up the listing in your Printify dashboard.

But before you hit publish, you will have several selections you will need to make:

Thumbnail: Printify offers pre-made mock-ups of your designs on products, eliminating the need for photography. Choose the image you want to be the thumbnail in your Etsy listing and deselect any photos you don't want for your listing. Note that you can also utilize mockups for your photos; we'll discuss this option later in this chapter.

Title: The title should be concise and accurately describe the product. It should include relevant keywords to help with search optimization. As an example, let's say you are listing a sweatshirt with a cat design on it. A good title would be *Unisex Cat Graphic Sweatshirt - Cute Feline Design Pullover - Soft and Comfortable Casual Wear.*

Description: The description should provide additional details about the product, such as the material, size, and care instructions. It's also a good idea to include a unique selling point or something that sets the product apart from others.

Using the cat sweatshirt example, a good description could be: *Stay cozy and show off your love for cats with this unisex graphic sweatshirt. Made with a soft and comfortable blend of polyester and cotton, this pullover features a cute feline design that will make you the envy of cat lovers everywhere. The classic fit and ribbed cuffs and hem provide a comfortable, casual look that can be dressed up or down. Machine washable for easy care. Available in multiple sizes, this sweatshirt is perfect for cat lovers of all ages. Order yours today!*

Notice how the keywords used in the title are also used in the description? That is part of optimizing Etsy's SEO or search engine optimization. Repeating these keywords in the title, description, and later in the tags tells Etsy that these are important keywords for your product, which will help your product rank higher in search when a shopper uses those keywords.

Variants: In a Printify draft, the *Variants* section refers to the different options available for a product, such as size, color, or style.

This section allows you to set up and manage the various options you want to offer to customers in your Etsy shop.

When setting up variants, you will typically choose the product you want to sell, set the price, and select the options available for that product. For example, for that cat sweatshirt, you might set up variants for assorted sizes (S, M, L, XL) and colors (black, navy blue, heather grey). Once the variants are set up, customers will be able to select their preferred size and color when they purchase the product in your Etsy shop.

Every product selected on Printify has a *Variants* section to complete. The number of options in this section depends on the product, with items like sweatshirts having more options for color and size, while simpler items like rectangular mousepads have only one option. In cases where there is only one size and color, the only field you will need to edit is the price you are charging.

PRO TIP: Top Etsy POD sellers create separate listings for each color of clothing, instead of listing multiple colors in the same listing. This allows the thumbnail photo to highlight only one color, making it easier for customers to find exactly what they are looking for. For example, a customer searching for a gray cat sweatshirt will be more likely to click on a listing that displays a gray sweatshirt as the thumbnail, rather than one that shows a blue sweatshirt with gray as an option only seen by customers who actually click on the listing.

Having separate listings for assorted colors of a product on Etsy can increase your visibility and help attract more customers to your shop. Although it will result in additional listing fees, the advantage of having multiple listings is that it increases the number of products you have available on the site and provides customers with a clear view of the options available. When a customer sees a product they like and clicks on it, they may browse your entire shop and discover other products they like. This can increase your chances of making a sale and growing your business.

Pricing: Now to one of the biggest decisions you will make when your list POD items for sale on Etsy: Pricing your products.

You will first want to research your competitors to see what they are charging for the same products you intend to sell. Note that you will want to try to come in slightly under their price, especially when you are just starting your shop. Remember that you can adjust prices at any time.

Before you set the price for your print-on-demand products on Etsy, it is important to determine the total cost of each item, including the cost from Printify and any additional expenses such as Etsy fees, design services, and graphics purchases. Use the pricing information provided by Printify to determine the cost per item and then use an Etsy fee calculator to calculate the total costs, including all fees. This will give you an accurate idea of your profit margins before settling on a purchase price for your products. Remember to consider the cost differences for assorted sizes of the same product and adjust the price accordingly.

I use an Etsy fee calculator every time I list a new item on Etsy to make sure my products will be profitable. Here are a few popular websites that offer free Etsy fee calculators:

- **FetchEtsyFees** (https://fetchetsyfees.com)
- **Etsy Fee Calculator** (https://etsyfeecalculator.com)
- **Merchant Mavericks** (https://merchantmavericks.com/etsy-fee-calculator/)

Variant Visibility: One of the biggest advantages of using Printify for your POD business is the fact that they have multiple print providers in its system. For popular items such as sweatshirts and coffee mugs, you will see the same product offered by more than one company. This allows you to pick the manufacturer with the highest rating and best price.

It's common with print providers for popular products to temporarily go out of stock, especially during the busy holiday season. If you have a product go out of stock, you can choose to have Printify fulfill the order by automatically selecting another supplier for that order. This is where the *Variant Visibility* option comes in.

The *Variant Visibility* option in Printify (and other providers) allows you to control the display of your product variants (e.g., different sizes, colors, etc.) on your Etsy shop. You have the option to show all variants, regardless of their availability, hide out-of-stock options, or show in-stock options as available and out-of-stock options as "sold out." Printify recommends, and most Etsy sellers agree, that you show out-of-stock options as "sold out" rather than hiding them completely.

Printify provides an option to automatically select another print provider for out-of-stock items. For instance, if your preferred print provider is unable to fulfill an order for a 2X sweatshirt, you can authorize Printify to choose an alternative provider to fulfill the order. However, it is not recommended that you opt for this approach. By allowing an alternate print provider to substitute your initial product choice with one of their own, you relinquish control over the product and provider quality. Your initial choice of sweatshirt may have been based on the ranking of your preferred printer. But if you allow for a substitute product, the subsequent option may come from a provider with an unfavorable rating.

Shipping Profile: The shipping profiles on Printify determine how your products will be shipped to your customers. This can be very confusing, especially when offering multiple products from different suppliers. Fortunately, most of the print providers, including Printify, offer default shipping options for every product, including every variation of a product, that will automatically sync to your Etsy listing. This means the customer will pay the exact shipping cost for every item and you don't have to worry about figuring out shipping charges.

When a customer purchases a print-on-demand item from your Etsy shop, they are charged by Etsy for the cost of the product as well as the postage. Etsy deducts its fees automatically and deposits the remaining total into your account, which is then transferred to your bank account. However, you are still responsible for paying the print provider the wholesale price of the item that you sold and the postage since they are the ones shipping the product to your customer. Even though the customer paid for the postage on Etsy, you are still obligated to pay the postage cost to the print provider. The amount left in your bank account after paying the print provider is your net profit.

Publish: The last step to launching your product on Etsy is to publish the draft you've created. By clicking the *Publish* button on Printify, they will immediately sync your product listing with your Etsy shop, making it visible and available for purchase by your customers.

It can take a few minutes for a listing to show up in your Etsy shop. But once it does, there are some edits you will need to make, which you can easily do by opening the listing in your **Seller Dashboard:**

Verify the correct category has been assigned: Etsy uses the product title to assign a category, but it may sometimes be incorrect. For instance, if you were listing Christmas tree skirts, which have a dedicated category on Etsy, but it was categorized under Women's Skirts, you will need to make sure that it is in the right category.

Select colors: You will need to manually choose the primary and secondary colors of your item. The color fields are optional, but it's recommended to fill them in to enhance the visibility of your listings in both Etsy and Google searches.

Select an occasion: The occasionfield is optional. It allows you to specify if your product is appropriate for a particular event or celebration. Occasions cover events such as birthdays, weddings, and baptisms.

Select a holiday: If your product is associated with a specific holiday, you can select it from the list of available options. This field is also optional. Holidays are set occasions that are recognized by an entire region, such as Christmas, Mother's Day, or Father's Day.

Renewal options: For your POD products, it's recommended to set automatic renewal rather than manual. If you choose manual renewal, the listing will expire after four months, and you'll need to go back to your POD provider's dashboard to relist the item. This can result in a loss of ranking and starting over from scratch if the product has been performing well.

Production partners: When running a print-on-demand store, it's crucial to accurately list all the companies you've acquired graphics from. Your POD print provider will automatically be listed, but it's your responsibility to manually include any other sources you use in your business, such as Creative Fabrica and Canva. Unless you created your designs entirely on your own, your listings should have at least two production partners.

Failure to enter the correct production partners can have legal implications and result in your business facing copyright issues. Additionally, it can also impact your search ranking and visibility on Etsy, as the platform prioritizes listings that follow its guidelines and regulations. It is important to accurately list all of your production partners to maintain the integrity of your business and ensure a successful POD store on Etsy. Buyers won't see the names of the companies you list, only that you are using third-party companies to complete the production of your products.

Section: Organizing your Etsy shop into sections or categories is vital to improving both the shopping experience for your customers and your Etsy SEO. It reinforces the keywords you have included in your title, description, and tags and signals to Etsy their importance for search engines. You can edit and rearrange your sections at any time. I like to alphabetize my shop sections. For POD, create your sections based on the theme, target audience, or occasion. For example, if you have a coffee mug shop, your sections might include "Mugs for Moms," "Mugs for Dads," "Mugs for Nurses," etc.

Tags: Tags in an Etsy listing are keywords or phrases that describe the product and help customers find the product in search results. These tags are used by Etsy's search engine to match the product with relevant search queries and help to increase the visibility of the product in search results. It is important to choose relevant, descriptive tags to maximize the listing's visibility and help customers find your product more easily.

Etsy allows you to enter up to 13 tags in each listing. Each tag has a limit of 20 characters.

Let's say you are selling a Mother's Day coffee mug. Examples of tags could be:

1. Mother's Day gift
2. Mom gift
3. Coffee mug
4. Mother and child
5. Mother's love
6. Personalized mug
7. Mother's Day present
8. Mother daughter gift
9. Mom birthday gift
10. Best Mom ever mug
11. Mother's Day mug
12. Mother's love mug
13. Gift for Mom

Again, make sure you add tags that you've also used in your title, description, and shop section to increase the chances of your item being found in the search. As I've mentioned already, I use sites such as **eRank** and **EtsyCheck** to research keywords and tags for my listings.

Materials: There are usually two materials sections in Etsy listings. The first is for selecting the materials used in making the item, and these options are pre-defined based on the category of your item. The second section allows you to manually enter the materials used. This second section is located under the tags section. Both materials sections are optional.

Personalization: If you are offering to customize your POD products, you will want to select *Personalization* in your listing. Etsy will then offer a field for buyers to enter their requests. You can edit this field with exact instructions for customers.

Publish: Once you've made these additional edits to your Etsy listing, you will click *Publish.*

And that's it! Your POD item is now officially for sale on Etsy!

From here, you simply repeat the process. I like to do batch work when I am listing POD items. I will create my drafts in Printify, completing 10 like items (for example, working on cat-themed computer mouse pads only) and publishing them in bulk to Etsy. I will then go over to Etsy and use their bulk editing feature to add categories, sections, and tags. This makes the entire listing process go much faster than if I edited every single listing individually.

How many listings do you need to build a successful POD shop? Some sellers try to list several items per day. With POD, the more items you list, the better chance you have of making sales. Most full-time POD Etsy shops have several hundred, if not a thousand listings. I recommend starting slow with the goal of one new listing every day. This will help you learn at a slower pace while also getting new listings up. As you become more comfortable with the process, your listing speed will increase. And then it's only a matter of how big of a shop you want to have!

Mockups: Note that one of the biggest things you can do with your Etsy listings is to add additional photos beside or in place of the ones your printer provider supplied. Most POD sellers employ the use of mockups for this purpose.

Mockups are digital representations of your designs placed on products, unlike the built-in images offered by print-on-demand companies. Using mockups instead can enhance your product presentations and help you stand out on Etsy, especially in highly competitive categories like clothing. Having unique and appealing images, especially in your thumbnail photos, can give you a competitive advantage.

It's crucial to use mockups that match the specifications of the products you are selling. This includes details such as the brand of the sweatshirt, to ensure that the mockup accurately represents the product you are offering. Many mockup providers list the product specifications they are using, making it easy to match them to your products. For example, if you are selling a specific brand of tee shirt, you can find mockups using that brand.

It's also important to ensure that the proportions of the graphics on the mockup are accurate. This includes the placement of the design, as well as its size concerning the product. You want the graphic on the mockup to be placed exactly where it will be when the customer gets their order.

There are many websites where you can obtain mockups. Some of the most popular are:

- **Creative Market**
- **Placeit**
- **The Mockup Club**
- **Pixelbuddha**
- **Graphic Burger**

You can also hire graphic designers through websites such as Fiverr and Upwork to create custom mockups for you. And you can also find Etsy shops that sell mockups. Remember, Etsy POD shops are extremely popular, meaning there are entire Etsy shops devoted to helping POD sellers grow their businesses.

Do you need mockups for your products? Honestly, that's a personal choice. Search Etsy for the type of products you plan on selling. If you are starting a tee shirt shop, search "tee shirts" on Etsy, find the shops with the most sales, and look at their photos. If they are using mockups, you may consider doing so, too.

In the beginning, however, I think using the pre-made mockups from Printify and sites like Printful is fine. It's better, in my opinion, to focus on starting your POD shop and becoming comfortable with the process of researching, designing, and processing orders. After you are confident in those steps, you can look into mockups. You can adjust your Etsy photos at any time, meaning you can also go back and upload new photos even after the listing goes live.

CHAPTER SEVEN: FULFILLING ORDERS

While you may hear online gurus try to sell you on the idea of an Etsy print-on-demand business being one where you earn passive income without you ever having to lift a finger, the truth is quite different. While POD allows for the automation of production and fulfillment, it still requires effort and attention to detail in areas such as product creation, marketing, customer service, and order management.

Indeed, you won't have to manually package orders with a POD shop. You won't have to invest in shipping supplies, print mailing labels, or take packages to the Post Office. Just as the creation of your products takes place entirely on your computer, so does fulfilling orders. So, in that way, it is a much easier business model than traditional retail. However, top Etsy POD shops do keep a close eye on the fulfillment of their orders.
While you can automate the fulfillment process for your Etsy POD orders through Printify, Printful, or most other print-on-demand printers, I strongly recommend that you manually process each order as it comes in, especially when you are just starting. While this is an extra step you will need to take when you get an order, it is very quick and easy to do. When I sell an item on eBay, it can take me up to 30 minutes to pack and ship it. With Etsy POD, it takes me less than a minute to fulfill an order.

As I've already mentioned, in my opinion, Printify is the best company to start your POD Etsy journey. Therefore, I'll use them to explain how they fulfill orders. With Printify, you have the option to choose automatic fulfillment through Printify without my intervention. I can set the fulfillment time to either within an hour or 24 hours, or I can manually push through all orders if I prefer.

As for me, I manually push through my orders on Printify. One reason for this is that sometimes customers want to cancel their orders, and this often happens within the first hour or two after placing the order. If I had automatic fulfillment enabled and missed the cancellation request until after Printify started processing the order, I would either have to decline the cancellation request or bear the cost of stopping the order. Because POD on Etsy is so competitive, I try to be as accommodating as possible to customers. I am fine with canceling an order before it is sent to production. But if I allow orders to manually be fulfilled, I may miss their deadline.

It's important to note that if you're selling customized items in your Etsy POD shop, you'll need to turn off automatic fulfillment. This is because you'll need time to upload personalized graphics to the items that your customers have ordered. If automatic fulfillment is enabled, the order will start processing before you've had a chance to upload the customized graphics, meaning you will have to cancel the order and resubmit it, paying for the product that Printify already sent to production.

Here are the steps to fulfill an Etsy order through Printify:

1. Login to your Printify account.
2. Check the new order notification and go to the *Orders* section.
3. Click on the specific order and review the details.
4. If it is a custom order, upload the personalized graphic and apply it to the product before submitting it for production.
5. If the order is not custom, simply submit it for production.

In my experience, I prefer to process my Etsy POD orders manually within two hours of receiving the customer's order. This allows the customer enough time to cancel if needed, while also ensuring prompt production of the order. Once the production of the order has started, I reach out to the buyer on Etsy to inform them that their order is being processed and provide an estimated delivery date. I also inform them that the tracking information will be automatically uploaded to their Etsy account once the order is shipped.

Do I have to take the additional step of communication with my customer? No. Since I don't offer personalization, there is no need to communicate directly with my buyers. However, because the processing and shipping times for POD are longer than if I was shipping the item myself, I want to make sure my buyers understand that their order isn't going to be shipped out that day or even the next. Yes, the processing and shipping times are detailed in the listing, but the truth is that most people don't read the listings of the products they order. They order based on the photos they see.

As you continue growing your Etsy POD shop, you may eventually decide to allow Printify or whatever print provider you use to automatically process orders. If you choose that option, I highly recommend you select the 24-hour option so that you will still have time to cancel orders if necessary.

PRO TIP: Large POD shops schedule all orders to be processed at the same time every day. This is so their credit card will be charged once per day versus multiple times per day, which can trigger a fraud alert on most credit cards. These sellers also schedule daily Etsy payouts so that they can pay off their credit card balances daily to ensure they don't go over their credit limit.

CHAPTER EIGHT: CUSTOMER SERVICE

Your Etsy POD shop is up and running. Hopefully, orders are coming in and you are continually adding new products. However, just because your business is completely online, you will still have to deal with customers. And that brings us to one of the most frustrating aspects of running a business: customer service.

Handling customer service issues is part of owning a business, whether it is online or off. The fact is that no matter how hard you try, you can never please all the people all the time. Eventually, you will likely have a customer complain about an order. Maybe it arrived later than promised or doesn't match their expectations. And with POD, there can be more customer issues than if you were shipping the product directly to customers.

Having physical products on hand allows you to verify their quality and gives you control over when they are shipped. However, with POD, these two critical steps are beyond your control. Although many POD companies maintain high standards for quality control, errors can occur. Longer processing times also mean a longer shipping time, and most POD items are shipped using economy (i.e., the slowest) shipping options, which significantly lengthens the time it takes for customers to receive their products.

When it comes to handling customer service issues on Etsy, the first step is to avoid them in the first place. You can do this by ensuring your listings are accurate. With POD products, this means that you want to make sure all details about the product are in the description along with your policies.

For instance, if I list a print-on-demand shirt in my Etsy shop, I ensure that the product information includes the size chart, material, and washing instructions. Additionally, I specify in the description that the shirt is a custom product and is only produced and shipped upon order placement. I clearly state that I do not accept returns or exchanges, and my store policies reflect this policy.

Does that mean I never get return requests? Unfortunately, no. I recently had a return request because a customer ordered two items when she only wanted one. Because this was an error on the part of the buyer and not me nor my print provider, I politely turned down the request, pointing out my shop's policies both in the listing description and in the ordering section.

However, in another case, the processing time for an item went past what was stated in the listing. This was during the busy holiday season, and the printer was behind on orders. In that case, I did cancel the order. Fortunately, in that case, because the printer was at fault, they absorbed the cost of the canceled order.

With POD products, it's also possible that items do not arrive as described due to a printing issue. Perhaps a graphic appears off-center, or the color didn't print correctly. If a product is defective, that is on the print provider. You will either need to have the printer remade and resend the item; or, if the customer prefers, refund them outright. In both cases, the print provider may want the customer to return the defective item to them. Or they may ask for photos to show the item was defective. Either way, it will be up to you to coordinate the refund or return process. Your customer will not be able to communicate directly with the print provider; that job is solely on your shoulders.

Blocking a Customer: I have been selling online since 2005, and I always joke that 99.9% of my customers are great. It's just the .1%

that drives me crazy. When dealing with difficult customers, do your best to remain calm. Many customers face issues with online sellers regarding problems with their orders, so sometimes they start aggressively expecting a fight. However, if you keep your composure and show sympathy for their situation, it will help settle them down.

Sometimes, however, buyers become angry and take it out on you, the seller. And while a seller can't block a customer on Etsy, if you are experiencing issues with a particular customer, you can contact Etsy's support team for assistance. The support team may be able to guide how to handle the situation, or they may act on your behalf if necessary, including removing the buyer from the platform if their behavior is violating Etsy’s policies. Etsy has access to messages between customers and sellers, so if someone is using inappropriate language or threatening you or your business, Etsy will take action.

Handling Bad Reviews: If an Etsy customer leaves you a false or misleading review, you can contact Etsy's support team to report the review and request that it be removed. To do this, you will need to provide evidence that the review is false, such as a copy of a conversation with the customer or evidence of the transaction. Etsy's support team will review the situation and take appropriate action, such as removing the review or issuing a warning to the customer.

To **contact Etsy support**, follow these steps:

1. Go to the Etsy website and scroll down to the bottom of any page.
2. Under **Help** click on the **Help Center** link.
3. This will take you to the **Etsy Help Center** page, where you can find a variety of articles and tools to help you manage your shop.
4. Scroll down to the bottom of the page.
5. You will find a link to **Contact Support** or **Get help with a specific issue.**
6. Click on either link, and it will direct you to a new page where you can select whether you need help as a buyer or as a seller.

7. You will be asked to select a specific topic or issue that you need help with.
8. You will be provided with an option of phone, email, or live chat support depending on the availability.

PRO TIP: Fear of dealing with angry customers keeps many people from even starting an Etsy shop. However, in all my years of selling online, I can count on one hand the number of problem customers I have had. I am proactive in avoiding customer issues by ensuring my listings are accurate, and that my policies are clearly stated, and by professionally handling customer issues. Even if a customer sends me a nasty message, I take a deep breath and respond professionally and do my best to de-escalate the situation. Do the same and you will keep any customer issues to a minimum!

CHAPTER NINE: MARKETING & ADVERTISING

When you begin the process of starting an Etsy shop, one of the first things you will hear is the term SEO. SEO refers to the practice of optimizing your online content so that it is more visible and easily discoverable by search engines like Google. When done effectively, SEO can help your products to rank higher in search results and increase the chances of them being seen by potential customers.

Sounds technical and complicated, doesn't it? Well, it's not. The fact is that **SEO boils down to the use of keywords**. We covered this earlier in this book regarding setting up your Etsy listings. Using the same keywords in your listing titles, descriptions, tags, and even shop sections is what will help your items not only rank high in Etsy's search but also outside of Etsy on search engine sites such as Google.

While utilizing keywords to help items rank high in search is important on every e-commerce website (not only Etsy but also Amazon, eBay, Poshmark, etc.), it's especially important on Etsy as the Etsy algorithm expects the keywords to repeat in various places. In contrast, it's usually enough to load an eBay listing title with keywords and not worry about repeating those keywords anywhere else within the listing. The same is true for Poshmark. Even Amazon, which has its own set of tags sellers can enter when listing an item, isn't as dependent on this multilayer keyword strategy.

Is having to research relevant keywords and then make sure you repeat them several times within the same Etsy listing annoying? Yes. Will you be tempted to ignore Etsy SEO and just list items quickly using whatever keywords come to mind? Yes. Will you be able to organically grow your Etsy POD shop without SEO? No.

The fact is that you NEED to focus on Etsy SEO to build and grow your business.

But while SEO is a huge part of customers finding your products when they are searching Etsy or Google, there are other things you can do to bring traffic to your Etsy shop. And fortunately, most of these things are not only relatively easy but also free. That's because these tactics mostly involve utilizing social media platforms to grow your business.

When e-commerce was still in its initial stages, there were very few shopping websites and customers were limited in where they could buy things online. When I began selling online, the only online retailers were eBay and Amazon. For years, I sold on both sites successfully. Because customers only had these two websites to shop on, I didn't have to compete for shoppers. The customers came to me because they didn't have anywhere else to go.

However, the e-commerce landscape has changed significantly since I began my online selling career. There are now thousands of online shopping websites available, including Etsy. This increase in competition means that simply listing products for sale is no longer enough to make sales. Etsy is an especially competitive marketplace, with POD shops dominating the platform. Therefore, sellers must actively seek out buyers and take steps to differentiate themselves from the competition to attract customers.

It's important to think of your Etsy shop as a brand. The niche you focus on, the products you choose for your shop, and the aesthetic of your products should all have a cohesive look and theme that contributes to your brand identity. If your products have a boho theme, you'll be using early tones as your color scheme that attracts a younger, trendy crowd. If like me, you focus on retro-themed items, you'll have bright pop art designs that appeal to baby boomers and GenX.

Once you know your target customer base on Etsy, you will need to go off of Etsy in search of more customers. And the first place you will want to start is on Facebook.

Facebook: If you want to grow a successful Etsy shop of any kind, creating a Facebook page is necessary. With nearly 3 billion registered users, there's no better place to find new customers than on Facebook. And it's free and easy to do so when you set up a Facebook Page for your business.

Some Etsy sellers opt to use their personal Facebook page as their business page, but I disagree with this approach as you want to keep your personal and business lives separate. A personal Facebook page allows users to add you as a "friend," while a business page requires users to "like" the page to follow it.

By setting up a dedicated business page on Facebook, you can create a professional online presence for your business and reach a wider audience. After all, you can't depend on your friends and family to be your only customers; you will need to extend your reach to find customers who not only like your products but will buy them.

You can use a Facebook business page to promote your products, share updates about your business, and interact with your customers. It is easy to link to your Etsy shop on your Facebook page so that users can easily access your listings. By building a following on Facebook and actively engaging with your audience, you can drive traffic to your Etsy shop and increase sales.

To create a Facebook business page, follow these simple steps:

1. Go to facebook.com/about/pages
2. Log in to your personal Facebook account
3. Follow the prompts to create a new business page

The first decision you will need to make is to name your page. I currently have several Facebook pages, including one for my Etsy Shop. My Facebook page name is Jean Lee Publishing, which matches my Etsy Shop name.

As you create additional social media accounts related to your Etsy business, it's important to make sure that they all have the same name to establish a cohesive online presence. You will want all your social media account names to match or closely match your Etsy shop name.

There are many ways to personalize your Facebook business page to make it unique and reflective of your brand. Some options include:

1. **Adding a profile picture:** This is the main image that will appear next to your page name and posts. I advise that you use the same profile picture for your Facebook page that you use for your Etsy shop.
2. **Adding a banner:** This is the large image that appears at the top of your Facebook page. You can use a custom banner that you have designed or made on a site like Fiverr.com, or you can create your graphics using tools like Canva or WordSwag. Just as you want your profile picture to be the same across your Etsy shop and all social media accounts, it's also a good idea to make your Facebook banner match or closely match the one in your Etsy shop.
3. **Customizing your page's tabs:** Facebook allows you to add various tabs to your page, such as an events calendar or a shop tab. You can customize these tabs to suit your business and make it easier for users to find the information they are looking for.

It's important to complete the **About** section on your Facebook business page to provide visitors with information about your business. This can include details about your products and services, your business history and mission, and your contact information. However, since this is a business page and separate from your page, it's important to be mindful of the information you share.

For example, while you may want to include your phone number on your page so that friends and family can contact you, it may not be appropriate to include it on your business page unless you have a brick-and-mortar location that you want customers to visit or call. For an Etsy POD shop, your entire business is online through Etsy. Therefore, there is no need for anyone to call you.

Page Category: Several categories may be relevant for an Etsy POD shop on Facebook, and Facebook allows you to select three. I recommend the following:

1. **Shopping & Retail:** This category is for businesses that sell physical products, such as clothing, coffee mugs, and home décor.
2. **Arts & Crafts:** This category is for businesses that sell handmade or creative products, such as stickers, jewelry, or prints.
3. **Gifts & Specialty Items:** This category is for businesses that sell unique or specialty items, such as custom products, and those targeting special occasions and holidays.

It's important to choose three categories as that will help to ensure that your Facebook page is visible to as many people as possible and that users can easily find and follow your page. You can also change categories at any time if necessary.

Once you've chosen your page's categories, you will want to personalize your Facebook business page by editing the URL to reflect the name of your page. Remember that you want to name your page the same as your Etsy shop or close to it. This will make it easier for users to find and follow your page, as well as establish a cohesive online presence.

To **change the username** of your page, follow these steps:

1. Go to your Facebook page and click on the **About** tab.
2. Click on the **Edit** button next to the **Page Info** section.
3. Scroll down to the **Username** field and click on the **Create** button.
4. Enter the desired username and click **Save.**

Once you have saved your username, your Facebook URL will be updated to reflect the name of your page. You can share this URL with customers and promote it on your other social media platforms and online listings to drive traffic to your Facebook page and increase engagement with your brand. A simple method for this is to simply direct people to find you on Facebook using the @ symbol. For example, my Facebook page is @jeanleepublishing. Entering @jeanleepublishing into the Facebook search bar will take you directly to my page.

The **About** section of your Facebook page has two description fields: a **Short Description** and a **Long Description**. The *Short Description* is a brief overview of your business, while the *Long Description* provides more detailed information.

- Use the *Short Description* to provide a brief overview of your Etsy shop, such as the exact types of products you offer, your target audience, and what your niche or theme is. Keep it concise and to the point, using keywords that accurately describe your business. For example, "Discover unique and personalized bridesmaids' gifts at our Etsy shop! From custom tote bags to monogrammed jewelry, we have everything you need to show your bridesmaids how much you appreciate them. Shop now and make your wedding day unforgettable!"
- Use the *Long Description* to provide more detailed information about your business, such as your history, values, and unique selling points. This is a good place to share your Etsy journey, explain why you started your business, and what your long-term goals are. For example, "Welcome to our Etsy shop, where we specialize in providing beautiful and thoughtful gifts for bridesmaids. Whether you're looking for something custom, monogrammed, or just plain special, we have everything you need to make your bridesmaids feel loved and appreciated. We understand that your wedding day is one of the most important days of your life and that the memories you make with your bridesmaids will last a lifetime. That's why we've created a unique collection of gifts that are not only functional but also stylish and memorable. From custom tote

bags to monogrammed jewelry, we have everything you need to show your bridesmaids how much you care. Each gift is crafted with love and attention to detail, ensuring that you and your bridesmaids will treasure them for years to come. So why wait? Shop now and make your wedding day unforgettable! With our wide selection of gifts, there's something for everyone, and you're sure to find the perfect items to show your bridesmaids just how much they mean to you. Thank you for choosing our Etsy shop, and we can't wait to help you create lasting memories on your special day."

In addition to filling out the *About* section of your Facebook business page with information about your Etsy shop, you can also use the **General Information** field to share links to your other social media accounts.

To **add links to your other social media accounts** (which we will discuss later in this chapter), follow these steps:

1. Go to your Facebook page and click on the **About** tab.
2. Click on the **Edit** button next to the **Page Info** section.
3. Scroll down to the **General Information** field and click on the **Add a Website** button.
4. Enter the URL of your social media account and click **Save.**
5. Repeat the process until you have added links to all of your pages.

You can add links to as many social media accounts as you like, including Instagram, Twitter, Pinterest, YouTube, and more. It's important to note that you should **put the address to your Etsy shop in the main Website field**, as your primary goal is to drive traffic to your Etsy listings.

One way to make it easy for users to shop your Etsy listings from your Facebook business page is to add a **Shop Now** tab with a call-to-action (CTA) button. This will create a direct link to your Etsy shop, allowing users to easily browse and purchase your products.

To **add a Shop Now tab to your Facebook business page**, follow these steps:

1. Go to your Facebook page and click on the **More** tab at the top of the page.
2. Select **Manage Tabs** from the drop-down menu.
3. Scroll down to the **Add a Tab** section and click on the **Add a Button** button.
4. From the list of options, select **Shop Now** as the type of CTA button you want to add.
5. Enter the URL of your Etsy shop in the **Webpage Link** field and click **Save**.

The *Shop Now* tab and CTA button will now appear on your Facebook business page, allowing users to easily access your Etsy listings and make purchases. You can customize the text and appearance of the CTA button to match your branding and create a cohesive look and feel for your page. And you can change these settings at any time.

The **Settings** tab on your Facebook business page allows you to control how users can interact with you and your page. This can be particularly useful if you have stringent privacy settings or want to limit the types of interactions you receive.

To **access the Settings tab**, follow these steps:

1. Go to your Facebook page and click on the **Settings** tab at the top of the page.
2. From the left-hand menu, select **Messages** to manage your messaging preferences.
3. Under the **General** section, you can choose to allow or block users from messaging you and whether or not you want to receive notifications when you receive a new message.
4. You can also choose to allow or block users from posting on your page and whether or not you want to receive notifications when you receive a new post.
5. Scroll down to the **Blocking** section to block specific users or groups from interacting with your page.

By adjusting the settings on your Facebook business page, you can control how users can interact with you and manage the types of interactions you receive. Keep in mind that you can always change these settings later if your preferences change.

Once you have set up your Facebook business page, you need to start building your audience by getting people to "like" your page. One way to do this is to invite friends and family to your page to "like" your new business page, as most of the people you are connected with will give your page a follow. However, remember that you can't expect your friends and family to buy from you. To build a business, you need to reach beyond your immediate circle.

While creating a Facebook business page is free, there are some paid options that Facebook offers to help grow your business. Facebook Ads allow you to target specific groups of people who may be interested in your products and encourage them to "like" your page to click through to your Etsy shop.

To create a Facebook ad:

1. Go to your Facebook business page and click on the **Create** button at the top of the page.
2. From the drop-down menu, select **Ad** to create a new ad campaign.
3. **Choose your ad objective.** Facebook offers a range of ad objectives to choose from, including "Website Visits," "Conversions," "Product Catalog Sales," and more. I recommend "Website Visits" because, after all, the goal is to bring customers to your Etsy shop.
4. **Set up your targeting options.** Facebook allows you to target specific groups of people based on demographics, interests, behaviors, and more. Use the targeting options to narrow down your audience to the people most likely to be interested in your products. You can do this by typing in keywords that relate to your products.
5. **Select your ad placements.** You can choose to show your ad on Facebook, Instagram, or both, as well as on other platforms such as "Audience Network" and "Marketplace." I choose all options so that my ad has the widest reach.

6. **Set your budget and schedule.** Decide how much you want to spend on your ad campaign and over what period. You can choose to run your ad continuously or set specific start and end dates. I usually start with $5 a day to test the ad.
7. **Create your ad.** Use the ad creation tools to design your ad, including the ad format, images, text, and call-to-action (CTA) button. You can choose from a variety of ad formats, including single images, carousels, and videos. I recommend adding a few of your best-selling product photos.
8. **Review and submit your ad.** Once you have finished creating your ad, review all the details to make sure everything is correct. When you are ready, click **Submit** to create your ad campaign.

The **Boost Post** feature on Facebook is a paid advertising tool that allows you to promote a specific post from your Facebook business page to a larger audience. This is an easier method than creating an ad from scratch.

To **boost a post from your Facebook business page**, follow these steps:

1. Go to your Facebook business page and find the post that you want to promote.
2. Click on the **Boost Post** button below the post.
3. **Select your target audience.** You can choose to show your boosted post to people who already like your page, to a specific group of people based on demographics and interests, or to a custom audience that you define. I usually choose to have the post shown to people who like my page and their friends and family. This way the people they are connected to will see that their friend or family member likes my business, which can encourage them to check it out.
4. **Set your budget and duration**. Decide how much you want to spend on your boosted post and over what period. You can choose to boost your post for as little as $1 per day or as much as you want. I like to choose a seven-day option with a budget of no more than $35 ($5 per day) to test how the ad performs.

5. **Review and boost your post.** Once you have finished setting up your boosted post, review all the details to make sure everything is correct. When you are ready, click **Boost** to promote your post.

So, you have set up a Facebook page for your business and have started getting people to "Like" it. Now what? Providing helpful content on your page will be vital to keeping it up to date and attracting new followers.

I share my newest listings directly to my Facebook page, as Etsy makes this incredibly easy to do. To **share an Etsy listing on your Facebook page**, follow these steps:

1. Go to your Etsy shop and find the listing that you want to share.
2. Click on the **Share** button below the listing.
3. Select **Facebook** from the drop-down menu.
4. A pop-up window will appear, asking you to log in to your Facebook account. Enter your login credentials and click **Log In.**
5. A new window will appear, allowing you to customize the message that will be posted to your Facebook page along with the listing. You can add a message or simply leave the default message.
6. When you are ready, click **Post to Facebook** to share the listing on your Facebook page.

In addition to promoting your listings on Facebook, it's a good idea to engage with your followers and keep them informed about your business. You can do this by posting updates about new product launches, your best-selling products for a particular week or month, or other relevant information such as deadlines for holiday orders. Creating polls about new product ideas is another clever way to create engagement. Note that when people engage with your Facebook posts, Facebook may show the engagement in that person's feed so that their friends can see it. And those friends, seeing that they know someone who follows your page, may decide to follow your page, too.

It's important to keep your posts positive and avoid posting about controversial or offensive topics. In other words, unless you are selling religious or political-themed products, avoid those two topics. The goal of your business page is to attract customers and make money. Posting about sensitive subjects can potentially turn people away. It's better to stick to topics related to your business and save the personal commentary for your personal page.

That's not to say you can't post more personal, lighthearted content on your Facebook business page. Sharing a picture of your lunch while you take a break from designing or posting a meme related to your niche can often bring more engagement than posting a new listing.

Facebook Group: As your business grows, you may decide to create a special Facebook group just for your Etsy shop customers. I have a Facebook group for my Etsy sticker shop that lets me connect with my best customers. They help me narrow down new sticker designs, and I reward their loyalty with special discount codes.

To **start a Facebook group:**

1. Log into Facebook and navigate to your business page.
2. In the top right corner of your page, click the **Create Group** button.
3. Select either **Close** (a private group that only members can access), **Secret** (an even more private group that only members can see and that doesn't appear in search results), or **Public** (a group that anyone can see and join). I have my group set to private so that Facebook users can see it but only members can see what is being posted. Since I post exclusive discount codes in the group, I want to make sure only members can see those posts.
4. Choose a **name and description** that accurately represents your business and the purpose of the group. I recommend selecting a name that matches up with your Etsy shop. My Etsy sticker shop is "Jean Lee Publishing," and my Facebook group is "Jean Lee's Sticker Club."

5. You can **invite members** by searching for Facebook users, adding email addresses, or inviting members from your business page.
6. You can **customize group settings** such as who can post and comment, who can see the group, and who can be added as a member.
7. When you're ready, click the **Create** button to launch your group. You can start posting updates and engaging with members right away.

It's hard to start a group until you have people following your Facebook page. And having a group isn't a necessity for any business. But as your business grows and you build up a loyal customer base, it may be something to consider.

Twitter: Like Facebook, Twitter is another popular and free social media platform that can be useful for promoting your Etsy business. With Twitter, you can share short updates, called "tweets," with your followers and engage with them through @replies and hashtags.

If you don't already have a Twitter account, you can create one for free at Twitter.com. Alternatively, if you have an existing personal account that you are active on, you may want to consider creating a separate account for your Etsy business to keep your personal and professional lives separate.

Remember as you are creating social media pages for your Etsy shop It's a good idea to use the same handle for your Twitter account as you have for your Etsy shop to create a consistent online presence for your business. This will make it easier for people to find and follow you across different platforms and helps in building your brand identity.

Twitter limits their "tweets" to 280 characters or less. Etsy makes it easy to share your listings on Twitter by including a share button in all active listings. To use the Twitter share button, simply click on it within a listing, and a new window will open on Twitter with the title of your listing and the direct link to it already populated. You can send the "tweet" as is or customize the message as well as add hashtags.

Hashtags (marked as such with the # sign) are a way to categorize and organize content on social media platforms, especially on Twitter. In fact, I find that hashtags are more useful on Twitter than on any other platform. Users can follow their favorite hashtags to keep up with the posts they are most interested in seeing.

Adding hashtags to your "tweets" can be an effective way to increase the visibility of your posts and reach people who are looking to buy the products you sell. By adding relevant hashtags to your tweets, you can make it easier for people to discover your Etsy business and perhaps buy your items.

For example, let's say your Etsy POD shop focuses on coffee mugs. When you click on the Twitter icon in the listing, your title and the link to the listing will automatically populate to Twitter. If there is room to add more text, you may consider adding hashtags such as #etsy, #etsyshop, #coffeemugs, and #mugs. If the mug is for a specific occasion or holiday, add hashtags to represent those events. These hashtags will help your tweet show up in searches for these topics, meaning they will show up for Twitter users following those hashtags.

It's worth noting that it's important not to overuse hashtags or use ones that are not relevant to your business. This can make your tweets seem spammy and could turn people off. Instead, choose around five relevant hashtags that accurately describe your business and the products you are selling. While the bridal category is huge on Etsy, don't use the hashtag #bridal in your listings if you sell pet items.

As with sharing your Facebook page with customers, you also want to share your Twitter handle, both online and offline, to encourage them to follow you on the platform. Including your Twitter handle in your other social media profiles and on business cards or other promotional materials will help your customers find you.

One way to build up your followers on Twitter is to follow other users and engage with their content. Some users follow everyone who follows them, which can help increase your follower count. You can also use Twitter's @reply and retweet features to engage with other users and share their content with your followers. This can help build relationships and expose your content to a wider audience.

PRO TIP: You want to connect with other Etsy sellers on Twitter. However, avoid connecting with other POD shops (unless they sell completely different items than you do) as this creates unnecessary jealousy and competition. Instead, search the hashtag #etsyshop and follow users whose products you like. Most Etsy sellers love to connect with shops that aren't in direct competition with their own. Promote their shops by retweeting their posts and they may do the same in return, which will help you potentially attract new customers.

Just like on Facebook, you can use Twitter to send and receive messages from other users. On Twitter, these messages are called **Direct Messages,** or **DMs** for short. You can send DMs to any user who is following you, and you can also receive DMs from users who you follow. Or you can block messaging.

In addition to messaging, Twitter also allows you to create **Lists** to group users you follow into categories. Lists are a useful way to organize and keep track of the accounts you follow, and they can also be used to create customized feeds of tweets from specific users. For example, you might create a list of "customers," "Etsy shops," "POD," or "print on demand" to help you stay organized and focused on the content that is most relevant to your business.

Instagram: Like Facebook, Instagram is a social media platform that allows users to share photos and videos and engage with their followers. There are several features on Instagram that you can use to share your content about your Etsy POD shop:

- **Instagram Posts:***Instagram Posts* are static photos that you share on your profile. They are visible to all your followers and remain on your profile indefinitely unless you delete them. *Instagram Posts* are an effective way to share high-quality images that represent your business and highlight your products, so be sure to only use your absolute best product photos when sharing.

- **Instagram Stories:***Instagram Stories* are photos or videos that you share on your profile that disappear after 24 hours. *Instagram Stories* are a good way to share ephemeral content, such as behind-the-scenes glimpses of your business, sneak peeks of new products or other engaging content that you want to share with your followers but that you don't want to remain on your profile indefinitely. You can also share your static posts to your story to make sure it gets maximum exposure.
- **Instagram Reels:***Instagram Reels* is a feature that allows users to create and share short video clips of up to one minute and thirty seconds that can be edited with music, effects, and other creative tools. *Instagram Reels* is a good way to create and share fun, creative content that engagingly highlights your products or business.

In addition to using Instagram to promote your Etsy listings, you can also use the platform to connect with your customers on a more personal level by sharing photos that may not always relate directly to your business. This can help you build a stronger connection with your audience and give them a more well-rounded view of your business. To achieve this, you can share photos of your office, pictures of designs you are working on, and other behind-the-scenes glimpses of your shop.

You can also share photos of your pets, meals, or other interests to give your followers a more personal look at your life. It's important to keep in mind, however, that you are using Instagram to promote your Etsy shop. Just as with your other social media business pages, you should avoid sharing controversial or offensive content.

Just as you use hashtags on Twitter, they are also a useful tool on Instagram. Here are a few tips for using hashtags effectively on Instagram to promote your Etsy shop:

1. **Use relevant hashtags:** Make sure to use hashtags that are relevant to your business and the content you are sharing. This will help ensure that your posts are seen by users who are interested in what you are selling. As an Etsy POD shop, stick to hashtags related to the niche and products you are selling.

Many people will use hashtags that have nothing to do with their Etsy shop to be seen by more users. But this can backfire if those users are annoyed seeing your content in their feed and react negatively by leaving mean comments under your posts.

2. **Use a mix of popular and niche hashtags:** Using popular hashtags can help increase the visibility of your content but using too many popular hashtags can make it harder for your content to stand out. Consider using a mix of hashtags to balance visibility and relevance. For example, you want to use the hashtags #etsy and #etsyshop in most of your Instagram posts. But also add hashtags of the theme of the products you are posting about. If you are sharing your listings of Father's Day coffee mugs, use hashtags such as #dad, #fathersday, and #giftsforhim to reach people who follow those specific tags.
3. **Don't overdo it:** Using too many hashtags can make your content look spammy and may turn off some users. Aim to use around five hashtags per post to strike a good balance between visibility and relevance. A tip is to create a list of hashtags in the notes or memo section of your smartphone that you can simply copy, paste, and edit when you are creating a new post.

Unlike other businesses where you would use hashtags of your business model (for example, I have an Etsy sticker shop, so I often use the hashtag #etsystickershop), with POD you aren't going to use that term or any that relate to selling print-on-demand items as hashtags. Rather, you will focus on using hashtags of the products themselves along with the niches you are targeting. Not only are most customers not familiar with the terms *POD* or *print-on-demand*, but using them can bring other POD shop owners to your listings and create unnecessary competition.

Narrowing down the hashtags you want to include can be a challenge as there are so many potential options. For instance, if you are selling personalized Christmas ornaments, you could choose from numerous hashtags, including:

- #etsy

- #etsyshop
- #christmas
- #etsychristmasshop
- #christmasornaments
- #personlizedornaments
- #customerornaments
- #personazliedgifts
- #personalizedornaments
- #christmasgifts
- #holidaygifts
- #giftsforher
- #giftsforhim
- #giftsformom
- #giftsfordad
- #ornaments

Linking Your Shop: You cannot add a live link to your Etsy shop in static Instagram posts, meaning the URL won't be clickable for users. However, Instagram allows you to include one live clickable website link in your profile, which you can use to link to your Etsy shop.

To drive traffic to your Etsy listings on Instagram in static posts, you can share photos and include a message in the caption that directs your followers to your profile page, where they can find an active link to your Etsy shop. For example, you can write "Brand new Mother's Day gifts are now available in our Etsy shop! Follow the link in our profile @yourinstagramaccount to shop now!"

By including the @ symbol and your Instagram handle, you will create a clickable link that will take users to your profile page, where they can click on the link to your Etsy shop and browse your listings. You can create a live clickable link in your Instagram stories, however using the **Link** option.

If you want to share multiple links on Instagram, you will need to use a service like **Linktr.ee** to create a landing page that allows you to list all your links in one place. When you create a *Linktr.ee* page, you can add as many links as you like, and users will be able to access them all by clicking on the main *Linktr.ee* link in your Instagram profile. To see an example, visit my *Linktr.ee* page at **linktr.ee/anneckhart.**

As with Twitter, you'll want to connect with other Etsy sellers on Instagram. However, try to avoid other POD shops as the market is too competitive and you don't want to create a target on your shop from other shop owners. Instead, search out the hashtags #etsyshop and #etsyseller to find accounts that aren't selling POD products such as vintage and craft sellers.

Pinterest: Pinterest is a social media platform that allows users to share and discover ideas and inspiration by "pinning" images and videos to virtual boards. As with Facebook and Twitter, Etsy includes a share button in all active listings that makes it easy to share your listings on Pinterest. By sharing your Etsy listings on Pinterest, you can increase the visibility of your products and potentially drive traffic to your shop, especially if your items have a cohesive look and are targeting a specific niche.

You can share your Etsy listings on specific boards that you have created, such as a "Christmas" board or a "Gifts for Men" board. I recommend starting a board that coincides with every one of your shop's sections. As with the other social media platforms, you can use hashtags to make it easier for people to discover your Pinterest boards, although hashtags aren't used as much on Pinterest as they are on other sites.

Finding content on Pinterest that coordinates with your products and re-pinning those posts as well as following their creators is a free and easy way to connect with other accounts. However, as we've already discussed, avoid other POD content as you don't want to create unnecessary competition. Rather, search for content that relates to your niche. For instance, if you sell wedding-themed products, follow boards about wedding planning. If you sell pet products, follow boards about dogs and cats.

If you do become active on Pinterest, be sure to share your Pinterest account with your customers and followers on other social media platforms and any promotional materials. You can easily add your Pinterest account to the links section of your Facebook page.

TikTok: TikTok is a social media platform that allows users to create and share short, lip-sync, and comedy videos. TikTok began with a younger demographic but is slowly growing with users of all ages. On TikTok, users can create short videos (up to three minutes) that can be edited with music, effects, and other creative tools. From comedy skits and dances to personal stories and small business, there are TikTok videos for every interest.

Since TikTok relies on short-form videos, it can be challenging to come up with content related to your POD business. After all, your products are being sold by a third party; you won't have most of your products in hand to highlight in videos. You will need to use images and create your videos, which you can do on a site like Canva. Or you can make sure you always have sample products on hand to show in videos.

There are two types of TikTok accounts users can create: personal or business. A TikTok personal account is a type of account that is used by individuals for personal use, such as sharing content with friends and family, connecting with others with similar interests, and expressing their creativity.

A **TikTok business account** is a type of account that is specifically designed for businesses to use on the platform. Business accounts on TikTok have access to features and tools that are not available to personal accounts, such as analytics, advertising, and the ability to create and manage ads.

The biggest benefit of a TikTok business account is that you can put a clickable URL in your profile. I have my Linktr.ee link in my TikTok business account profile, which will take people to a static page with all of my business links, including a link to my Etsy shop.

If you want to use TikTok to promote your Etsy business, you definitely want to create a TikTok business account. Note that you can create multiple TikTok pages within one account; if you already have a personal account, you can easily add a second business account. It’s easy to switch back and forth between your multiple accounts without having to constantly log out and back in.

To create a TikTok business account for an Etsy shop, you will need to follow these steps:

1. **Download the TikTok app** on your phone or tablet.
2. Open the app and tap on the **Me** icon in the bottom right corner.
3. Tap on the **three dots** in the top right corner and select **Manage account**.
4. Tap on **Switch to Professional Account**.
5. Select **Business** as the account type.
6. Follow the prompts to complete the account setup process, including adding your business name, contact information, and any other required information.

Once your account is set up, you can start creating and sharing content to promote your Etsy shop. Keep in mind that TikTok may require you to verify your business account before you can access all the features and tools available to business accounts. This may involve providing additional information or documentation to prove that you are the owner of the business.

There are several ways you can use TikTok to promote your Etsy business:

Create and share posts about your products: Use TikTok's creative tools and features, such as music, effects, and filters, to create short, entertaining videos that highlight your products creatively and engagingly. Order product samples to use in videos or use your mockup photos set to music to create short, engaging posts.

Participate in trends: TikTok is famous for trending dances, challenges, and filters. Participating in these is a fantastic way to create engagement. While the trends may not have anything to do with your business, because they are so popular, your posts are bound to get more views. A good rule of thumb is to post one business post for every three fun posts. Make sure to only participate in trends that are non-controversial and won't harm your business image.

Use relevant hashtags and tags: By including relevant hashtags and tags in your TikTok posts, you can make it easier for users to discover your content and interact with your account as well as hopefully visit your Etsy shop. However, as we've already discussed, unlike other Etsy shops, you aren't going to use any hashtags relating to your business model. For example, you don't want to use the hashtags #POD, #printondemand, or #dropshipping. It is okay, however, to use the hashtags #etsy, #etsyshop, and #etsyseller. Add additional hashtags that relate directly to your niche and products.

You can also try searching for hashtags related to specific themes or categories, such as #weddings or #gifts. Additionally, you can use TikTok's search function to discover more hashtags related to your specific niche. Searching for the hashtag #weddings will lead you to the trending bridal hashtags. And when you discover new hashtags, you will also find new targets to create products for.

As I mentioned in the Instagram section of this chapter, I keep a list of hashtags in the notes section of my phone that I just copy and paste into posts. TikTok allows you to write up to 2,200 characters in the caption of a post. However, it's worth noting that captions on TikTok are usually short and attention-grabbing, as the main focus is on the video content rather than the text. A caption of around 100-200 characters is considered optimal for TikTok, as it allows for enough text to add context and engage with the audience, but still keeps the focus on the video.

Utilize TikTok's advertising features: TikTok's business accounts have access to advertising features that can help you reach a wider audience beyond those who follow your account and drive traffic to your Etsy shop. You can create and manage ads on TikTok to reach users who are interested in your products or related topics based on their activities on the app, which TikTok tracks. TikTok's advertising opportunities include:

- **In-feed ads:** These are native ads that appear in users' feeds, like sponsored posts on other social media platforms. They can be in the form of videos, photos, or carousels and can include a call-to-action button.
- **Brand takeover ads:** These are full-screen ads that appear when a user opens the app. They can be in the form of a video or image and are a great way to grab users' attention.
- **Branded hashtag challenge:** This feature allows businesses to create a hashtag challenge, which encourages users to create and share content using the designated hashtag.
- **Branded effects:** TikTok's AR effects allow businesses to create their own branded filters and lenses that users can use in their videos.
- **Branded hashtag stickers:** These are branded stickers that users can use in their videos and are associated with a specific hashtag.

To access TikTok's advertising platform, you will need to sign up for a **TikTok Ads account**. Here's how you can do that:

1. Go to the TikTok Ads website at **tiktok.com/business/ad-center**.
2. Click on the **Sign-Up** button in the top right corner of the page.
3. Fill in the required information to create a new account, including your name, email address, and password.

Once you have created your account, you can access TikTok's advertising platform by logging in to the TikTok Ads website and clicking on the **Create** button in the top right corner of the page. From there, you can choose the type of ad you want to create and follow the prompts to set up your campaign.

Etsy's Marketing Tools: While social media is a fantastic way to build your POD brand and stop, Etsy itself offers several marketing tools to help sellers promote their products and reach potential customers.

Some of the marketing tools available on Etsy include:

Shop Announcements: This feature allows you to create a message that will be displayed on your shop's homepage and in the emails you send to your customers. You can use this feature to announce sales, new products, or other important updates about your shop. Here are some ways you can utilize this feature to promote your POD shop:

1. **Share new product releases:** Use your shop announcements to let your customers know about new designs or collections that you have released.
2. **Highlight popular products:** If you have any products that are particularly popular and are selling well, consider using your shop announcements to give them some extra visibility.
3. **Share your story:** Use your shop announcements to give your customers a behind-the-scenes look at your business and share your personal story. You can talk about your inspiration for your products, your creative process, or anything else that you think would be of interest to your customers.
4. **Offer promotions and discounts:** Use your shop announcements to offer promotions or discounts to your customers. This can be a great way to drive sales and encourage customers to purchase from your shop.
5. **Keep your customers informed:** Use your shop announcements to keep your customers informed about any changes or updates to your shop, such as new policies or shipping times, especially during the busy holiday season.

Shop Blog: This feature allows you to create a blog within your Etsy shop where you can share news, updates, and other information about your products and business. You can use the same ideas as noted in the *Shop Announcements* section in the blog area.

Etsy Ads:*Etsy Ads* allow you to create targeted ads that will be displayed to potential customers who are searching for products like yours on Etsy. To **create an ad for your shop on Etsy**, go to your Seller Dashboard and click on the Marketing tab. Click on Etsy Ads. Choose a daily budget anywhere from $1 to $100.

Etsy Offsite Ads: This feature allows you to place ads that will be displayed on other websites and platforms, such as Facebook, Instagram, and Pinterest. For sellers with less than $10,000 in the yearly sale, Etsy *Offsite Ads* are an optional program one needs to opt into. However, it is mandatory and automatic for shops that sell over $10,000 a year. You only pay for an offsite ad if it leads to a sale. You do not pay if someone clicks on the ad but does not make a purchase.

You can end your *Offsite Ads* at any time unless you are automatically enrolled due to selling over $10,000 a year. There is no way to end or opt out of *Offsite Ads* for those sellers. While this may seem unfair, to be honest, if you are selling over $10,000 a year on Etsy, *Offsite Ads* should be affordable for you. Again, you only pay if the click on an ad leads to a sale.

To access the **Offside Ads** section of your account, go to your **Seller Dashboard** and click on the **Settings** tab. Then click on **Offsite Ads.**

Free Shipping Guarantee: If you are charging customers for shipping, you can opt into Etsy's *Free Shipping Guarantee*, which is where customers get free shipping on orders of $35 or more. Etsy will show customers that they can get free shipping in your shop when they order $35, which can help increase your average sale order total.

If you are charging for shipping, Etsy will frequently prompt you to consider their *Free Shipping Guarantee*. Otherwise, you can find it under **Settings:Shipping settings** in your **Seller Dashboard.**

Be sure to take your costs into account before opting for the free shipping guarantee. As we've already discussed several times, the margins on POD products are tight. Running sales and offering free shipping will only further cut into your profits. Fortunately, Etsy will prompt you to raise your prices to account for free shipping. But make sure you are always checking your numbers to ensure you aren't losing money.

Sales & Discounts: You can create various sales and discounts for both new and returning customers. You will find the **Sales &**

Discounts section under the **Marketing** tab in your Etsy dashboard. You can offer several types of discounts, including:

- **Percentage off:** You can offer a percentage off the purchase price for a specific product or the entire order. For example, you could offer a 10% discount on all tee shirts in your shop, or a 20% discount on orders over $50.
- **Amount off:** You can offer a fixed amount off the purchase price for a specific product or the entire order. For example, you could offer a $5 discount on all tote bags in your shop or a $10 discount on orders over $100.
- **Free shipping:** You can offer free shipping on a specific product or for the entire order. This can be an effective way to encourage more sales and reduce cart abandonment.
- **Sale events:** You can create a sales event by offering a discount on a selection of your products for a limited time.

Some of the offers you can send include:

- **Thank you:** Invite up to 200 recent customers back with a thank you offer by sending them an offer to show appreciation and encourage them to shop again. You can choose a discount amount of a percentage off, a fixed amount off, or free shipping with an order minimum.
- **Favorited item:** Turn favorites into orders by sending offers to anyone who favors one of your items. You can choose a discount percentage or a fixed amount off. Note that there is no minimum order option for the *favorited item* offers; it applies to a single item that someone has put into their cart.
- **Abandoned cart:** Remind shoppers to check out by sending an offer when someone leaves an item from your shop in their cart. As with *favorited items*, you can choose a discount percentage or a fixed amount off; and there is no minimum order amount as the offer applies to a single item that someone has put into their cart.
- **Run a sale:** Set lower prices for your whole shop or select categories. Many professional Etsy sellers will tell you that you should always be running sales and that your sales should

be short-term for no longer than 48 hours. This is because Etsy will show shoppers a countdown clock of the remaining time in a sale, which can create a sense of urgency. These sellers typically run the same sale every two days.

PRO TIP: Again, be careful with offering any discount or exclusive offer. The truth is that most Etsy POD sellers raise their prices over what the market rate is so that they can always have their items "on sale." And they often run short-term sales of 48 hours or less so that Etsy will show customers a count-down clock to encourage them to shop before the sale ends. Is it frustrating to have to play this "sale" game to get orders? Yes. But it is a fact of the retail industry. People buy more items when they are on sale. Making sure you know your numbers so you can play the discount game will help you sell more items. Before offering any type of discount, use an Etsy fee calculator to figure out your costs.

Create a promo code: Etsy allows shops to create a custom code to send to customers directly. You will need to enter a code name, a description of the offer, and the discount amount. You can also choose to set an expiration date and a minimum purchase amount. You can manually end your coupon codes at any time.

Etsy does not distribute these coupon codes; that is something you need to do. If you have a mailing list or Facebook group, you can share special promo codes with them. I have a Facebook group specifically for my Etsy shop and frequently share special promo codes just for them.

Product reviews: If you are struggling to grow your POD business, you might consider reaching out to social media content creators to see if they will feature your products in a YouTube video, TikTok, or Instagram post. Note that if the person has a large following that they will charge for such a service, and often this cost is too much for a beginning shop owner to afford. However, smaller creators who are trying to get their platform off the ground are usually open to receiving free items in exchange for a review. Or you might collaborate with another Etsy shop owner (again, someone who isn't in your niche) to exchange products where you will both do reviews of the other's products.

Blog/Website: Creating a blog or dedicated website can be a great way to build a stronger connection with your customers and establish your POD brand. By regularly updating your site with posts about new inventory, you can keep visitors engaged and interested. This can be especially valuable if you plan to make your Etsy shop your primary source of income.

However, if your Etsy shop is only a hobby or part-time job, you may not need to create a dedicated website or blog. Instead, you can focus on promoting your products on Etsy directly as well as on the social media platforms we've already covered. If you do decide to create a website, you should consider whether you have the time and resources to maintain it regularly. Some things to consider when deciding whether to create a website include:

- Do you plan to author lengthy articles discussing the items you sell?
- Are you looking to use your site not just as a sales channel but also as a teaching tool? For example, if you sell bridal products, do you want to expand into articles about wedding planning?
- Do you want to sell products only through Etsy or do you plan to sell eventually and expand your brand to other online websites such as Amazon, eBay, or Shopify or at brick-and-mortar retail locations?
- Do you want to explore affiliate advertising or sell advertising on your site to earn extra money?

If you answered "yes" to any of the above questions, then you may want to consider starting a website. However, you will need to decide whether to go with a free blogging platform or a paid website. If you decide to go the paid route, you can invest in a sophisticated system or choose a simple, low-cost one.

Yes, there are lots of decisions to make when deciding whether or not to start a website!

There are several free blogging platforms available, such as Blogger and WordPress, that you can use to create a blog for your Etsy shop.

It's worth noting that Blogger is owned by Google, which means that you can apply for a Google AdSense account and place ads on your blog to generate additional revenue. In addition to driving traffic to your Etsy listings and increasing sales, a blog can be a useful way to monetize your online presence.

If you decide to create a paid website for your Etsy shop, it's important to do your research and choose a platform that meets your needs. Your Etsy shop should be the focus of your brand, with your blog or website serving as an additional tool to drive traffic to your listings. There are many low-cost website options available, such as GoDaddy.com and Wix.com, which offer not only URL registrations but also inexpensive hosting and simple website-building tools. Keep in mind that your goal is to drive traffic to your Etsy listings and increase sales, so choose a website platform that will help you achieve this.

If you expand the sale of your products on multiple websites in addition to Etsy, a blog or website can be a great place to provide links to those other platforms, such as Amazon, eBay, Shopify, or brick-and-mortar stores. A website can also help to establish your business as legitimate and build trust with potential customers, making them more likely to purchase from you than other sellers.

It's important to remember that maintaining your blog or website is just as important as creating it. In addition to posting regular updates, you should also make an effort to respond to any comments from visitors and ensure that all links are active and up to date.

If you are selling a large number of items on Etsy and plan to continue doing so as your primary business, you may want to consider registering for a domain name, which is a personal website address that is closely tied to your Etsy shop name. This can make it easier for customers to find and remember your website, as well as give you a professional online presence. You can purchase domain names through websites like GoDaddy.com and link them to your Etsy shop or other online platforms. For example, I have the domain **AnnEckhart.com** that directs users directly to my Amazon Storefront where all my books are listed. And **JeanLeePublishing.com** takes users to a website that directs them to my Etsy shop or my Amazon page for my stationery brand, both of which I use the same business name.

As you consider registering for a domain name, it's important to think about where you want the URL to direct users. Do you want people to go to your blog first, or do you want them to always go directly to your Etsy shop? It's important to remember that your blog or website should *complement* your Etsy shop, rather than serve as a replacement for it. So, unless you are selling products on multiple websites, you want your URL to point to Etsy.

If you are using a free blog on a platform like Blogger, you may want to choose a domain name that directs people directly to your Etsy shop, such as "MyStore.com", and keep the URL provided by Blogger for your blog as-is. Alternatively, you could choose a different domain name specifically for your blog, such as "MyEtsyShopBlog.com". The key is to choose a URL that makes sense for your business and helps to drive traffic to your Etsy shop.

In my opinion, it's important to have a personalized URL address that points directly to your Etsy shop, as your primary focus should always be on driving sales through Etsy. Your website should work to direct traffic to your Etsy listings, rather than intercept it. If you use the same name for your business on multiple online platforms, such as Amazon and Etsy, you may want to consider registering a domain name that reflects this.

If you do decide to start a website, you can earn additional income from ads and affiliate links. Amazon Associates is an affiliate program that allows you to earn money when someone buys a product through your link. And many of the design companies you will use in your POD business have affiliate programs you can join to earn even more money. Creative Fabrica, Canva, and Printify all have affiliate programs.

Mailing List: Creating a strong POD brand can lead to repeat customers who keep coming back to your store because they enjoy your products. To keep these loyal customers informed and engaged, you may want to consider setting up a mailing list. This can be a useful tool for staying in touch with your customers and providing them with updates about your business, such as new product releases, exclusive offers, and other important news. By building a strong relationship with your customers through a mailing list, you can foster customer loyalty and encourage them to continue shopping with you in the future.

Some popular mailing list services include:

- AWeber
- Campaign Monitor
- Constant Contact
- Drip
- GetResponse
- Mailchimp

These services provide tools for creating and managing email campaigns, including email design templates, subscriber lists, analytics, and automation features. Many also offer integrations with other marketing and sales tools, such as e-commerce platforms and CRM software. Most offer their services for free until you hit a certain number of subscribers, after which you will need to pay.

PRO TIP: If you do start to collect email addresses for a mailing list, make sure you keep a file of those addresses on your computer system, not only on the mailing list server. If you decide to stop using their service, you will lose those emails. Always make sure you have a backup so you can start a new list with another service if you decide to.

Note that many blogs and website platforms also have a built-in mailing list feature. For example, I have several websites through GoDaddy, all of which have a feature where visitors can enter their email addresses to join my mailing lists. Collecting email addresses will allow you to send newsletters, promotional emails, or other types of communications to your customers regularly to create brand loyalty and drive shoppers to your Etsy shop.

It's important to ensure that you are only sending emails to individuals who have specifically opted in to receive them, to comply with anti-spam laws, and to avoid annoying or alienating your customers. By providing valuable and relevant content to your subscribers and respecting their inboxes, you can build a strong and engaged mailing list that can help you drive sales and grow your business.

Putting It All Together: If you're feeling overwhelmed by all the different social networking sites and techniques, it's important to take things one step at a time. Start with Facebook, as it is the easiest and most effective. Then expand to Twitter, Pinterest, and Instagram, as you can stick to static posts on all of them. If you feel comfortable adding videos, you can expand to TikTok. Or just choose one to focus on, the one you most enjoy. Some Etsy shops only use Facebook, while others are solely focused on TikTok.

As you become more comfortable with each platform, you can gradually expand your social media presence and use these tools to promote your Etsy shop effectively. Just remember to take deep breaths and relax - there's no need to rush or feel overwhelmed. Rome wasn't built in a day, and neither were the top Etsy shops!

When you have an Etsy POD shop, your primary concern should be developing new products, creating listings, answering customer questions, and processing orders. A good title, photos, and description are crucial to creating an Etsy listing that will result in consistent sales. Think of social media as a bonus step in that listing creation process.

To promote your listings on social media, remember that you can use the "share" buttons provided by Etsy in every active listing. Simply click on the buttons for Facebook, Twitter, and Pinterest to share your listings on these platforms. As we've discussed, hashtags are incredibly useful to increase the visibility of your social media posts. Once you have connected your Etsy account to your social media networks, you can easily share your listings with just a few clicks and add a handful of relevant hashtags.

To avoid overwhelming your followers on Facebook with multiple listings at once, it is a good idea to share them individually over some time rather than all at once. This will help ensure that your followers see your posts and are more likely to click through to your listings. On Twitter and Pinterest, it is generally okay to share a larger batch of items at once, as these platforms do not have the same restrictions on business page posts. However, it is still a good idea to spread out your posts and mix in other types of content to keep your followers engaged.

To promote your business on Instagram, it is important to post regularly and engage with other users. Try to post at least a few times a week, if not daily. You can share photos of your office, new inventory, or even personal moments to give your followers a behind-the-scenes look at your business. Don't forget to include three to five hashtags with each post to make it easier for users to find you. And be sure to engage with other users by following them and liking their content. Spend a few minutes each day scrolling through your feed to connect with other users and discover added content. By posting regularly and engaging with your followers, you can build a loyal following and drive traffic to your Etsy shop.

If you have the time and resources to create and maintain a blog or website, this can be a great way to promote your Etsy shop. However, remember that they will require additional work and resources, so it's important to make sure they are worth the investment. If you do decide to start a blog or website, be sure to share it on your other social media accounts to get the most exposure. This can help drive traffic to your Etsy shop and increase sales. Just be sure to manage your time effectively and prioritize your efforts so that you can get the most benefit from your efforts.

PRO TIP: A great way to create one social media post that you can share across multiple platforms is to first film a TikTok video that is no longer than a minute and a half. You can then share that video on Instagram as a Reel. You can then share the Reel on your Instagram Story and Facebook. And if you have a website and mailing list, you can also post it there. This method gives you posts across all your platforms, and you only had to film ONE short video!

CHAPTER TEN: GROWING YOUR POD BUSINESS

As your print-on-demand business grows, you may want to explore selling options beyond Etsy. The good news is, most print providers offer integration with not just Etsy, but a multitude of other platforms as well. Before venturing into other sales channels, it is crucial to have a solid understanding of print-on-demand as a whole and a well-established Etsy shop.

However, once you are ready to branch out, both Printify and Printful offer seamless integration and make it easy to sell on other websites.

Printify: In addition to Etsy, Printify also integrates with the following websites:

- BigCommerce
- eBay US
- PrestaShop
- Printify API
- Shopify
- Squarespace
- Walmart US

- Wix
- WooCommerce

Shopify, WooCommerce, Wix, PrestaShop, BigCommerce, Squarespace, and the Printify API are all standalone websites that allow you to create a unique e-commerce shopping experience. Printify integrates with these websites in the same manner as it does with Etsy. To utilize these options, you need to set up an account on each platform. It is important to note that none of these sites are free to sell on. All come with fees.

Shopify is one of the most widely used platforms for businesses to establish their online storefronts. However, one of the major drawbacks of using Shopify and comparable sites is the requirement to handle payment processing, shipping, and sales tax collection and remittance for US states that mandate it. This can be a significant burden for businesses, particularly in terms of sales tax compliance.

While payment processing and shipping can be managed with relative ease, albeit with additional costs, the sales tax issue can often pose the biggest challenge for businesses creating their online storefronts. Platforms such as Etsy, Amazon, eBay, Poshmark, Mercari, and Walmart offer sales tax collection and remittance services on behalf of sellers, simplifying the process. On the other hand, if a business chooses to collect and remit sales tax on its own, it must obtain sales tax permits in every state that requires it, and different regions within those states may have varying tax rates. Sellers need to collect the tax and remit it to the relevant states quarterly, which is a significant and time-consuming endeavor.

It is certainly possible to eventually build your own e-commerce website for your POD brand as your business grows, especially if you can hire additional staff to assist you. However, the majority of POD sellers prefer to stay with platforms that offer support for payment, shipping, and tax collection, just as Etsy does. These platforms take care of complex administrative tasks, allowing sellers to focus on growing their businesses.

eBay Integration: When working with Printify, one of the top alternatives or compliments to Etsy is eBay. eBay is the third largest e-commerce platform in the United States, making it a logical choice for businesses looking to expand their reach once they have established their brand on Etsy. Integrating with eBay through Printify allows businesses to tap into a large and diverse customer base, increasing their visibility and sales potential. By leveraging the power of both Etsy and eBay, businesses can maximize their online presence and reach a wider audience.

The process of **integrating Printify with eBay** is straightforward and involves a few simple steps:

1. **Create an eBay account:** If you don't already have an eBay account, you'll need to create one. This is a free and easy process that is similar to setting up an Etsy account. You will need to have a credit card on file, enter your tax information (your social security number if American), and link your bank account to receive payments.
2. **Connect your eBay account with Printify:** You can do this by logging into your Printify account, going to the Integrations section, and selecting eBay. From there, you'll need to connect your eBay account to Printify. This is the same process as linking a Printify account to Etsy.
3. **Create your eBay listings:** You use the same process for eBay as you do for Etsy in that you create your listings on Printify and then publish them to eBay. As with Etsy, you will need to edit your listings on eBay to fill in item specifics.
4. **Launch an eBay store:** eBay offers store subscriptions starting at only $5. You get a set number of listings included with each store level. If you are going to list more than 250 items a month, an eBay Starter Store is the best option.

Just as Etsy has its own fees, so does eBay. From store subscriptions, listing fees, and final value fees, you can’t sell on eBay for free. However, just as Etsy handles payment processing, USPS shipping, and collects sales tax on the seller's behalf, so does eBay.

To learn more about how to sell on eBay, be sure to check out my book *Beginner’s Guide To Selling On eBay*, which is available on Amazon.

Walmart Integration: To link your Printify account to Walmart's website, you first need to apply to the Walmart Marketplace, which is a program for businesses in the United States, Canada, Mexico, the United Kingdom, Japan, India, China, and Hong Kong. U.S. sellers will need to submit several forms of business documentation, including various tax IDs. Selling on Walmart isn't for most Etsy POD shops as it is on an entirely different level. However, it is an option for those who want to significantly expand their business.

Printful: Printful offers more website integrations than Printify, including:

- Adobe Commerce
- Amazon
- Big Cartel
- BigCommerce
- eBay
- Ecwid by Lightspeed
- Gumroad
- Nuvemshop
- Prestashop
- ShipStation
- Shopify
- Square
- Squarespace
- Storenvy
- TikTok Shop
- Webflow
- Weebly
- Wix
- WooCommerce

While most of the options require you to provide your own website support for payment, shipping, and taxes, there are a few notable sites available on Printful, specifically Amazon, TikTok, and Gumroad.

Amazon: Amazon is the number one shopping website in America and many countries around the world. Amazon has a huge customer base, is a reliable and trusted website, is a highly searchable platform, and integrates seamlessly with Printful. On Amazon, you can reach more customers than all the other websites put together.

However, there are some **cons to selling on Amazon**, including:

1. **Competition:** Amazon is a highly competitive platform, with a large number of sellers, so integrating with Amazon means you'll be competing with other sellers for visibility and sales. POD products are exceedingly popular on Amazon with sellers from all over the world listing their products, many at rock-bottom prices. The money people earn on Amazon comes from volume, meaning you will have to sell more units of products at a lower price.
2. **Fees:** To start a Printful POD business on Amazon, you will need to pay for an **Amazon Seller Account,** which costs $40 a month. You will also be charged referral fees based on the category of your item and how much it sold for. And there are payment processing fees. Remember that all these fees are on top of Printful's fees.
3. **Complex requirements:** Amazon has strict requirements for product listings, such as product images, descriptions, and pricing, so it's important to familiarize yourself with these requirements before integrating with Amazon. For example, you may need to order samples of your products to take your own photos. And those costs add up quickly.
4. **Limited customization:** Amazon has strict guidelines for product customization, so you may be limited in terms of the branding and design options you can offer.

The fact that Amazon requires you to provide real-life product photos, not the images Printify provides, is the biggest hurdle to expanding your POD business to Amazon. However, if you end up scaling your business and begin manufacturing and fulfilling your orders (more on this in a bit), then Amazon becomes a better option.

TikTok Shops: In addition to Amazon, Printful also integrates into **TikTok Shops**. A *TikTok Shop* is a feature on the social media platform TikTok that allows users to set up an online store and sell their products directly to TikTok users. With TikTok shops, businesses can create a profile, upload product images and descriptions, and link to their website or other e-commerce platforms for checkout. Customers can browse and purchase products directly within the TikTok app.

TikTok Shops are part of TikTok's efforts to expand its e-commerce capabilities and provide businesses with a new way to reach and engage with customers. By setting up a *TikTok Shop*, businesses can tap into the platform's large and engaged user base, increase their visibility, and drive sales. *TikTok Shops* are still a relatively new feature, but they offer a promising opportunity for businesses looking to expand their online presence and reach a new audience.

Just as there are specific cons to selling POD on Amazon, there are some **cons to TikTok Shops**, including:

1. **Competition:** TikTok is a highly competitive platform, with a large number of businesses and creators selling products, so integrating with Printful for *TikTok Shops* means you'll be competing with other businesses for visibility and sales.
2. **Limited audience:** TikTok is primarily used by younger generations, so it may not be the best platform for businesses targeting older demographic groups.
3. **Limited customization options:** TikTok has strict guidelines for product customization, so you may be limited in terms of the branding and design options you can offer through your *TikTok Shop.*

In addition to paying the Printful fees for the price of the product and shipping, you will also pay fees on TikTok. TikTok charges fees for using its platform, including referral fees and transaction fees. The exact fees will depend on the pricing and payment structure set by TikTok, so it's important to familiarize yourself with these fees before integrating with Printful for *TikTok Shops.* It is also important to note that TikTok does take a percentage of sales for purchases made through *TikTok Shops*. The exact percentage will depend on TikTok's pricing and payment structure, so it's important to research and compare the fees and costs involved before integrating with Printful for *TikTok Shops.*

For more information on *TikTok Shops*, visit https://shop.tiktok.com/merchant/en.

Gumroad: Gumroad is an e-commerce platform that allows creators, artists, and entrepreneurs to sell their products directly to customers. The platform was created to make it easy for anyone to sell their products online, without having to deal with the complex technical and financial aspects of setting up and maintaining an online store.

Gumroad is primarily targeted toward artists, designers, writers, musicians, and other creative professionals who want to sell their digital products, such as eBooks, music, graphics, and other creative works. However, it's also used by entrepreneurs and small business owners who want to sell physical products, such as clothing, accessories, and other merchandise. The platform supports the sale of physical products through its integration with print-on-demand providers like Printful.

To start selling products on Gumroad, you'll need to create an account on their website. This will involve providing some basic information about yourself and your business. You will then need to connect Gumroad to Printful and begin adding publishing your designs to the site just as you do for Etsy.

While using Gumroad and Printful can be a fantastic way to expand your print-on-demand (POD) business, there are also some potential drawbacks to consider:

1. **Limited audience:** Gumroad has a smaller customer base compared to other e-commerce platforms like Amazon or Shopify, which may limit your potential reach and impact your sales.
2. **Competition:** Gumroad is a marketplace, which means that you'll be competing with other sellers for the attention of customers. This can make it more challenging to stand out and make sales, especially if you're selling in a highly competitive category.

3. **Fees:** While Gumroad and Printful are relatively low-cost options for starting a POD business, they do charge fees for their services. These fees can add up over time and impact your bottom line, so it's important to carefully consider the costs involved.
4. **Limited customization options:** Gumroad has limited customization options for your store and product pages, which can make it more difficult to create a unique and branded shopping experience for your customers.
5. **Shipping times:** As a POD business, you'll be relying on Printful to fulfill your orders, which can result in longer shipping times compared to other fulfillment methods. This may impact customer satisfaction and could lead to negative reviews or returns.

Uploading to Other POD Websites: So far in this book, the main focus has been on creating products using either Printify or Printful and integrating them with Etsy. However, there is another way to grow your print-on-demand business, which is to sell directly on print-on-demand websites. While you can expand your reach to other websites like Amazon and eBay by integrating your Printify or Printful accounts with those platforms, selling directly on POD websites is another option to consider.

That's right: Starting and growing a print-on-demand business doesn't necessarily require the use of a print provider like Printify or Printful, nor does it require selling on well-known platforms like Etsy. Instead, you can choose to upload your designs directly to POD providers who will handle the printing, shipping, and fulfillment of your products directly to customers, eliminating the need for integration with other platforms or having an Etsy account.

The process of selling your designs through print-on-demand providers is straightforward:

1. **Create an account:** Sign up for a free account with each POD provider you'd like to sell on.
2. **Upload your designs:** Upload your designs to the POD provider's platform.

3. **Select products:** Choose which products you want your designs to be printed on, such as t-shirts, hoodies, stickers, etc.
4. **Write a description:** Write a brief description of the item to help customers understand what they're purchasing.

And that's it! The POD provider will handle all customer inquiries, order fulfillment, and customer service issues, allowing you to focus on creating new designs. At the end of each month, the POD provider will send you a cut of the profits from the sales of your items.

No listing fees, no monitoring orders, no customer service? Sounds perfect, doesn't it?

Well, there is a catch.

While using these print-on-demand websites to sell your designs may seem like the perfect solution with no listing fees, order monitoring, or customer service required, it's important to keep in mind that these types of platforms typically receive a lot less traffic compared to well-known e-commerce sites like Etsy, eBay, or Amazon. This means that you may face a lower level of exposure and fewer sales opportunities compared to selling on these larger marketplaces.

However, if you want to grow your brand, slowly putting your best-selling designs onto the products these sites offer is a wonderful way to do so at no cost. These sites take their fees out, distributing your share to you directly. There are no invoices to look for and no bills to pay. It is the easiest way to sell POD items and is one of the most passive income models there is. After all, once you upload a design, that's it. You don't have to monitor your listings or manage anything. The only thing you'll see are the deposits into your account every month.

There are a lot of these POD websites out there; here are some of the best:

- Gearbubble
- Merch by Amazon
- Redbubble

- Society6
- Spreadshirt
- Sunfrog
- TeePublic
- TeeSpring
- Threadless
- Zazzle

Merch by Amazon: When it comes to selling graphic tee-shirts and sweatshirts, *Merch by Amazon* is more popular than Etsy. There are no fees to list products in a Merch by Amazon account, plus Amazon handles all the order processing, production, shipping, and customer service. And since Amazon is the largest e-commerce website in most countries, they have millions more customers than Etsy.

However, there are some drawbacks to *Merch by Amazon.* First, they only have a limited number of products, and all but two items are clothing. Second, their marketplace is extremely competitive. Millions of sellers are already using *Merch by Amazon,* meaning most products sell for much less than on other sites. The third and most significant is their system of tiers.

Merch by Amazon has different tiers or levels that determine how many designs a user can upload and how many products they can sell. The tiers are based on the number of products sold by each seller, and each tier has different limits and requirements.

Here are the different tiers on *Merch by Amazon:*

1. Tier 10: This is the starting tier for all new users. Users in this tier can upload up to 10 designs and sell them on Amazon.
2. Tier 25: After selling 10 products, a user can move up to tier 25. In this tier, users can upload up to 25 designs and sell them on Amazon.
3. Tier 100: After selling 25 products, a user can move up to tier 100. In this tier, users can upload up to 100 designs and sell them on Amazon.
4. Tier 500: After selling 100 products, a user can move up to tier 500. In this tier, users can upload up to 500 designs and sell them on Amazon.

5. Tier 1000: After selling 500 products, a user can move up to tier 1000. In this tier, users can upload up to 1000 designs and sell them on Amazon.
6. Tier 2000: After selling 1000 products, a user can move up to tier 2000. In this tier, users can upload up to 2000 designs and sell them on Amazon.
7. Tier 4000: After selling 2000 products, a user can move up to tier 4000. In this tier, users can upload up to 4000 designs and sell them on Amazon.

The higher the tier, the more designs a user can upload and the more products they can sell. However, users must maintain their sales volume to keep their tier level, or they may move down to a lower tier. This complicated process of limiting how many items you can list is in stark contrast to Etsy, eBay, and other websites where you can list as many items as you want.

Redbubble, TeePublic, TeeSpring, and Zazzle: Redbubble, TeePublic, TeeSpring, and Zazzle all stand apart from Merch by Amazon because they don't have design listing restrictions and offer a more extensive product range beyond just shirts. Although they don't attract as much customer traffic as Amazon, eBay, or Etsy, they present excellent opportunities to expand your print-on-demand (POD) business. By uploading your designs and choosing your products on these sites, they handle the marketing, printing, shipping, and customer service, paying you a percentage of the sales each month. These platforms offer a completely hands-free way to operate your POD business, and the profits you can make are passive.

PRO TIP: If you are thinking of expanding beyond Etsy and exploring other platforms, I recommend starting with my most popular designs and selecting one platform at a time. For me, I prefer TeePublic. Once I identify a top-selling design on Etsy, I upload it to TeePublic. Their platform features a broad range of products, which helps me extend my offerings beyond only tee shirts. Moreover, TeePublic offers a free listing service, so I don't have to be worried about accumulating additional fees. In case I have a design that I believe would work best on a t-shirt, I may also add it to Merch by Amazon.

Manufacturing Your Own Products: If you want to scale your POD business and take it to the highest level there is, you will be looking at manufacturing your products which you will then store and ship to customers yourself.

That's right: You can also choose to manufacture your products instead of using a print-on-demand provider! There are two ways to do this:

1. Order products from a printer that you will then store, fulfill, and ship.
2. Purchase the equipment needed to screen print your own products.

The advantage of manufacturing your own products is that you have full control over the quality of the products, as well as the cost and timeline for production. However, manufacturing your own products also comes with several challenges. You'll need to invest in the upfront cost of production, which can be substantial, especially if you're producing a large number of products. You'll also need to handle the storage and fulfillment of the products, which can be time-consuming and require additional resources.

Additionally, if you have a high volume of orders, you may need to invest in a larger space, hire additional staff, and purchase even more expensive equipment to handle the increased workload. After all, you aren't going to be able to print enough coffee mugs on your Cricut in a corner of your living room to grow a multi-million-dollar business.

If you do decide you want to start manufacturing your products to ship out yourself, you will want to start with ordering products you design in bulk. Many companies offer this service, including both Printify and Printful. If you have already been utilizing these companies for your Etsy POD business, it will be easy to simply place bulk orders to be shipped directly to you. You can also look into local printers in your area to see how their prices compare.

If you order products in bulk and are successful in selling them directly but want to cut costs by printing your products, you first need to source the raw materials such as blank tee shirts and sweatshirts then you can then screen print. You can purchase these products from wholesale companies, including:

- **Alpha Broder:** Alpha Broder is a wholesale clothing company that offers a wide range of blank shirts for screen printing, including t-shirts, hoodies, and more. They offer a variety of brands, styles, and colors to choose from.
- **Blankshirts.com:** Blankshirts.com is a wholesale clothing company that specializes in blank shirts for screen printing. They offer a wide range of t-shirts, hoodies, and more, from a variety of brands and in a range of styles and colors.
- **Next Level Apparel:** Next Level Apparel is a clothing manufacturer that offers a wide range of blank shirts for screen printing, including t-shirts, hoodies, and more. They offer a variety of styles and colors to choose from.
- **Royal Apparel:** Royal Apparel is a clothing manufacturer that offers a wide range of blank shirts for screen printing, including t-shirts, hoodies, and more. They offer a variety of styles and colors to choose from.
- **SanMar:** SanMar is a wholesale clothing company that offers a wide range of blank shirts for screen printing, including tee shirts, hoodies, and more. They offer a variety of brands, styles, and colors to choose from.

Obtaining wholesale products to screen print is just the first step of the process of printing your products. Screen printing requires a lot of special equipment and materials, including:

- **Screen printing press:** A screen printing press is the main piece of equipment you'll need. This is the machine that holds the screen in place and allows you to print your design onto the shirt.
- **Screens:** Screens are the frames that hold the stencil of your design. You'll need a separate screen for each color in your design.

- **Ink:** Screen printing ink is a specialized ink that is made for use in screen printing. You'll need to choose the right type of ink for the type of shirts you're printing on.
- **Squeegee:** A squeegee is a tool you use to spread the ink over the screen and onto the shirt.
- **Emulsion:** Emulsion is a light-sensitive substance that is used to create the stencil for your design on the screen.
- **Exposure unit:** An exposure unit is a machine that is used to expose the emulsion on the screen to light, creating the stencil for your design.
- **Washout booth:** A washout booth is a sink or basin that is used to wash out the emulsion from the screen after the stencil has been created.
- **Dryer:** A dryer is used to dry the shirts after they have been printed.

And don't forget about needing professional photography set up to take photos along with shipping supplies such as poly bags, tape, a thermal label printer, shipping labels, and digital scale to process orders.

Taking on your own screen printing is a lot, but some people have done it, converting a basement into their printing space, and partnering with a spouse or sibling to handle the business. However, this doesn't have to be your end goal. Plenty of people build their POD business exclusively on Etsy. Give your business a year or two to grow and evaluate where you are at. If you want to scale your business, start by expanding your listings to the sites mentioned earlier. The only thing limiting how far you want to take your POD business is your personal goals!

CHAPTER ELEVEN: ETSY ACCOUNTING MADE EASY

Let's be honest: Creating product designs and seeing sales come in is FUN! Bookkeeping and filing taxes are not. However, Etsy sellers are responsible for managing their accounting, including tracking their income and expenses and reporting their earnings to the appropriate tax authorities. Where you file taxes depends on the country you are running your Etsy shop from.

Managing your finances and taxes for your business can be done either by using software programs such as QuickBooks or by hiring a certified public accountant (CPA). While a CPA can handle the bulk of your bookkeeping, it is still necessary for you to perform some fundamental accounting tasks.

Thankfully, Etsy provides its sellers with a wealth of financial information to assist them in running their businesses. This includes comprehensive data on their sales, such as the total earnings, the number of items sold, and the average sale price. Etsy also provides information on expenses, including the fees paid to Etsy and the cost of any advertising or promotional campaigns run on the platform.

All this financial information is stored and updated in real-time in your account. From your **Shop Manager** dashboard, click on **Finances** to access the following:

Payment Account: The *Payment Account* section is where you can manage your payment and deposit information. To receive payment for the items you sell, it is necessary to link your bank account to Etsy. You have the option to choose your preferred deposit schedule from daily, weekly, every other week, or monthly transfers. As your POD business grows, you will likely want to choose daily deposits so that you can pay the credit card charges your print provider makes every time an order is placed.

Monthly Statements: The *Monthly Statements* section is, in my opinion, the most important part of the *Finances* area. In this section, you can access information about your sales, fees, marketing expenses, shipping costs, and net profit. You can view your monthly statements dating back to the beginning of your selling account. Regularly monitoring your net profit will give you an idea of whether you are making money or incurring a loss. Remember to keep in mind that the net profit displayed by Etsy does not take into account your offline expenses, such as inventory and shipping supplies.

QuickBooks for Etsy: For a fee, you can sync your Etsy seller account with *Intuit QuickBooks* to easily track your sales, expenses, and tax deductions.

TurboTax for Etsy: For a fee, you can sync your Etsy seller account with *TurboTax*, which can make filing your taxes easier.

Legal & Tax Information: The *Legal & Tax Information* section is where you will enter all the necessary legal information for your shop. This information is critical when it's time to file your taxes. Additionally, in this section, you will be able to download your 1099 form at the end of the year, which is required for tax filing purposes.

Fees: All selling platforms charge their sellers fees, and Etsy is no exception. Etsy charges fees to its sellers to cover the costs of operating the platform and providing services to its users. These fees include a **listing fee**, a **transaction fee**, and a **payment processing fee.**

The **listing fee** is charged whenever a seller creates a new listing for an item on Etsy. This fee is currently $0.20 per listing and is charged at the time the listing is created. Listings are active for four months and can be renewed by the seller at the end of that period for an additional $0.20.

The transaction fee is charged whenever an item sells on Etsy. This fee is currently 5% of the item's sale price, plus any shipping and gift wrap charges. The transaction fee is charged at the time the sale is made.

The **payment processing fee** is charged whenever a seller accepts payment on Etsy. This fee varies depending on the payment method used but is typically around 3% of the total transaction amount plus a fixed fee. The payment processing fee is deducted from the seller's account at the time the payment is processed.

Expenses: All businesses can claim business-related expenses as deductions on their taxes. With an Etsy POD shop, it's important that you carefully track your expenses, which will include:

- **Fees:** The fees charged by Etsy are automatically deducted from your account before your net profit is disbursed to you. If the fees and shipping costs are not specified on the tax form issued by Etsy, then you shouldn't need to report them during tax season. However, check with your CPA or tax preparer to be sure you are following the current tax laws for your area.
- **Cost of Goods:***Cost of Goods* refers to the amount charged by your print provider for each item you sell. For instance, if you only use Printify, you need to calculate the total amount they charged you during the year for every product you sold that they produced and shipped on your behalf.
- **Shipping costs:** While you won't have to carry a supply of boxes and shipping tape, you will have to reimburse the print provider for shipping costs. For example, every time you sell a tee shirt through Printify and they ship that shirt to your customer, they will add the cost of shipping to your account.

You will want to separate the shipping charges from the cost of goods charges for accounting purposes.

- **Advertising and marketing expenses:** Etsy will automatically deduct any charges for their ads, whether regular or off-site ads. However, if you advertise on Facebook or other social media websites, you will need to track those expenses. If you order extra products for giveaways or collaborations, you should be able to claim those costs under marketing.
- **Home office expenses:** If you run your Etsy POD shop from home, you may be able to claim a portion of your rent, utilities, and other home office expenses as a tax deduction.
- **Web Services:** Your biggest cost when it comes to running a POD business is typically graphic design services and subscriptions. This includes expenses such as monthly or yearly subscription fees for graphic design software and online platforms that you use to create and upload your designs. For example, I claim my subscriptions to Creative Fabrica and Canva under web services. In addition, you can claim the cost for websites you use for Etsy keyword research as well as costs from sites such as GoDaddy for URL and website hosting (if you have a standalone website).
- **Communications:** You can claim your internet service for a POD business. And if you use your smartphone for any business-related tasks, such as using design apps or tracking your shop through the Etsy app, you can claim that as well.
- **Business-related travel expenses:** If you attend trade shows or other events related to your business, you can claim the cost of transportation, lodging, and meals as a deduction.
- **Legal and professional fees:** This includes the cost of any legal or professional services you use in connection with your Etsy POD shop, such as accounting or tax preparation services.

Tracking your Etsy business expenses: There are several ways you can track your Etsy expenses to help manage your business and prepare for tax time. Here are a few options you can consider:

- **Use Etsy's built-in invoicing and payment tools to track your income and expenses.** These tools can help you keep track of the money you have earned, the fees you have paid to Etsy, and the expenses you have incurred in running your business.
- **Use accounting software to manage your finances.** There are many different accounting software options available, and some are specifically designed for small businesses or online marketplaces like Etsy. These tools track your income and expenses, generate reports, and prepare for tax time. TurboTax is the most popular of these services.
- **Keep detailed records of your income and expenses, such as receipts, invoices, and bank statements on a spreadsheet or even in a notebook.** Most of your POD income and expenses will be recorded online on Etsy, your credit card statements, your bank statements, and the print provider you use. This makes transferring that data to your computer or paper easy.
- **Hire a certified public accountant or professional tax preparer**. Turning to an expert to handle your financial management and tax preparation can be money well spent. In addition to filing your taxes, they can also provide expert guidance on managing your finances.

My Way: Etsy automatically deducts fees, advertising, and shipping costs from my account and only pays me the remaining balance, which is displayed under **Net Profit** in my Etsy account. At the end of the year, Etsy provides me with an annual 1099 form that lists my gross sales after all of their fees have been deducted. On my end, I only need to keep track of my deductions that occur outside of the platform, meaning I do not need to track my fees, shipping costs, or advertising expenses.

Your gross sales are your sales BEFORE any fees or expenses are taken out. On Etsy, they will show you your NET profit after they take THEIR fees, advertising, and shipping. However, as noted earlier, there are many more expenses you can claim as deductions when it comes time to file your taxes.

I use a basic spreadsheet to track my expenses every month. Every month I record my inventory costs (I use Printify exclusively, so this total is easy to find in my account), shipping charges (again, easy to find in my Printify account), advertising (since Etsy deducts their ads from my account, I only need to track if I run ads outside of their platform), home office expenses, web services (everything from Creative Fabrica and Canva to GoDaddy and EtsyCheck), communications (smartphone and internet), and professional fees (what I pay my CPA to file my taxes).

At the end of the year, I tally every category of expenses to get the year-end total for each. For example, I will add up all of the shipping costs for each month and enter that number into my year-end shipping field. Even though I have a CPA who files my taxes for me, I still provide him with these expense breakdowns so he can accurately file my returns.

At the end of January, I download the 1099 form from Etsy. I take that along with my list of year-end expenses to my accountant so he can file my taxes. Easy!

Disclaimer: Every state and country is different when it comes to taxes, so be sure to consult with a tax professional in your area for advice on how to manage your own Etsy bookkeeping.

CONCLUSION

I have had numerous online businesses over the years, everything from reselling vintage collectibles on eBay, running an Etsy sticker shop, filming YouTube videos, and, of course, authoring books like the one you are reading. But no business offers the same opportunity as an Etsy print-on-demand shop as it is accessible to almost everyone regardless of their station in life or skill level.

A POD business is one of the few "laptop lifestyle" business models that work. With just a computer and internet access, almost anyone can start a POD Etsy shop. Whether you draw your own designs or purchase ready-made graphics, sites such as Printify and Printful make it easy to put artwork onto products and sell them through Etsy. There is no inventory to carry or orders to package. You can run your business from anywhere in the world!

How successful you will be with an Etsy POD shop is up to you. If you follow the processes laid out in this book of research, design, and product selection, along with the listing and marketing tips, you can easily start a side hustle or grow a full-scale business. The choice is yours!

ABOUT THE AUTHOR

Ann Eckhart is a writer, entrepreneur, and online content creator based in Iowa. She has authored numerous books about home-based e-commerce businesses on topics including reselling, self-publishing, print-on-demand, and content creation. You can find all her titles at www.AnnEckhart.com.

◆ ◆ ◆

You can follow Ann Eckhart on the following social media platforms:

Facebook @anneckhart

Instagram @ann_marie_eckhart

YouTube @anneckhart

Made in the USA
Monee, IL
17 July 2023

39478770R00085